Oh, Baby

Stephen Church's "Four Early Lessons in Parenting" originally had a section appear in *River Teeth* under a separate title and is reprinted by permission of the author.

Terrance Flynn's "Baby Card" originally appeared in *Sycamore Review*, Fall 2014, and is reprinted by permission of the author.

Requests for permission to reproduce material from this work should be sent to:

Rights and Permissions
In Fact Books
c/o Creative Nonfiction Foundation
5501 Walnut Street, Suite 202
Pittsburgh, PA 15232

Cover and text design by Tristen Jackman

ISBN: 978-1-937163-21-1

Printed in the United States of America

Oh, Baby

TRUE STORIES ABOUT

Conception, Adoption, Surrogacy, Pregnancy, Labor, and Love

EDITED BY

Lee Gutkind AND *Alice Bradley*

WITH AN INTRODUCTION BY *Lisa Belkin*

InFACT
BOOKS
PITTSBURGH

Contents

Introduction

Lisa Belkin

My first son was a few days old, and I still hadn't surrendered to the new reality. The line between *then* and *now* is brightest in retrospect, and my mind hadn't figured out what my body had already guessed—that life was not the same. I still thought I was in charge, that I could make plans, that time was mine to control. Ha.

About a week or so into motherhood, I left the house with my baby—just the two of us for the first time. In preparation I fed him, changed him, dressed him, put him in his stroller, then gathered up a manuscript I was editing and navigated my way to a bench in the courtyard of our apartment building. It was a short walk, but suddenly everything along the way was either an obstacle or a threat. The dog down the hall, who'd been a friendly, galumphing creature just the week before, now looked downright menacing. The toddler he belonged to was no longer tiny but towering, his fingers full of germs. The elevator could get stuck. Or worse. The sky was too bright. But it also looked like rain.

Once through the gauntlet, my plan was to somehow rock the stroller with one hand and scribble notes with the other. I figured that yesterday he'd napped at this time, so that must be his pattern, right? Babies, I'd heard, were all about patterns. Also, there was work to be done, a remaining deadline from my receding life.

I had barely gotten my bottom on the seat when Evan began to cry. Wail, actually. Shriek and scream.

Maybe, with experience, I would have known that the sun was in his eyes, or his blanket was too heavy, or he was testing out his lungs, or sometimes babies just cry. Maybe, with experience, I'd have waited it out and not minded if people stared for a few minutes. I'd have understood that this would pass instead of feeling it to be a declaration that I was a failure as a mother. But Evan was the first baby I'd ever held, ever nursed, ever parented, and in that moment it felt as if nothing would ever pass. In the first weeks and months each everything was its own forever—every doubt, failure, realization, and revelation felt as though it had always been and would always be this way. He would cry into eternity. I would never write another word.

So I gathered up my things and I fled.

I wish, now, that I had lingered. Not just on that bench, but in that chapter. From my current perch, twenty-four years later, I realize that there is no forever in parenting—just blinks and hiccups, a staccato blur. Figure out one thing, and another challenge roars. You keep the balls in the air and the plates spinning and the feet stepping one in front of the other, and the days melt into nights, then dawn into days again. Every so often, during one of those dawns, you realize you are somewhere else entirely. Not in babyland but in toddlerhood, not new and unsure but confident—and now unsure about completely different things.

I am a writer. Looking back, I am stunned that I didn't write any of it down. That's the best way I've found to hold a moment—by putting pen to paper or words to screen, a permanent sketch for when memories fade. Yet I wrote almost nothing of those days, and now I recall them as though through a fog. When did he sleep through the night? How bad was the colic? Why can't I remember his first smile?

I wish I had written because then I'd have it captured, held in amber, sharp instead of fuzzy, real instead of hazy stories. And I wish I had written because, Lord, would it have helped. I am a writer because I think with my fingers; I make sense of my world during the pulses it takes to transfer a thought from brain to page. As a new mother, for the first time in my life— the only time—I was too enveloped by an experience to write about it, so it knocked me flat.

It would also have helped to read the writing of others. To have truly understood that this experience was not mine alone. But when Evan was born, that wasn't the way it was done. Parenting was still a silo, you and your experience parallel to but not touching all the others around you. You talked to friends, yes, sometimes, when you had the energy and inclination to be honest. You wrote in your diary, ditto, maybe. But the era of we-are-all-in-this-together had not quite dawned.

That is why I thrill to the new ways. And they are stunningly new—blogs and websites, an era of confession and counsel in which entire communities of strangers unite in capturing the moment and the message that no one is alone. A generation is letting their memories go out into the universe and, simultaneously, holding them tight. Memories and observations that would otherwise be lost to the haze of sleep deprivation and hormones are captured on a screen. In this world, affirmation, confirmation, sympathy, and advice are a page or a click away. It is imperfect, sure—don't get me started on some of the commenters—but its upside is exhilarating. (The rest of the commenters—*most* of the commenters—are wise and generous.)

You hold in your hand a result of this changed world. It's the kind of collection I wish had existed when I was in the thick of it. Filled with confession and compassion, chronicling all of it, making it clear that the early days are both singular and universal. When Elizabeth Anne Hegwood describes kissing her infant son's "velvet hair," willing him to stay a sweet baby; when stay-at-home mom Erin White confesses the unexpected "rage and loneliness" she feels at the sight of her wife getting dressed for work; when KC Trommer recalls the love, sublime but also common, she feels upon first seeing her son—they speak to me. They speak for me. They speak to and for us all.

Editor's Note

Alice Bradley

> "Making the decision to have a child—it's
> momentous. It is to decide forever to have your
> heart go walking around outside your body."
> —Elizabeth Stone

You may have heard this quote before. Maybe you've used it yourself. I heard it before I was a parent. I know that it was pre-parenting because I remember regarding it as if from a great distance. It seemed like a curious but probably accurate insight. *Sounds reasonable*, I thought. *You love your child, who is indeed, once born, outside the body. Sure, I can see that.*

Then I slept until noon and went out for a long brunch. I imagine. I can't remember much about those days, but what I do remember involves brunch.

Years later, as a new mother, I heard this again, this heart-outside-the-body quote. I understood it at that moment, absolutely and completely. I saw how unbearably tender an idea it is, and how horrific. *Oh my God,* I thought. *Heart outside the body? This is a terrible idea. This is unsound, medically and in every other way! What have I done? Is it too late to take it back?*

It turned out it *was* too late to take it back, and no matter what happened from that point onward, I was forever changed. When my child was born, another birth was happening, right there in the room, to both me and my husband: we became parents. No one gave us an Apgar score, but I'm sure we wouldn't have scored as highly as our son. No matter.

Given how overwhelming and bewildering new parenthood can be, it's no wonder that there are 86 billion (approximately) baby books out there. The moment we're handed another human being and told, "Here, you look like you could keep this alive," many of us run to a book—or an entire library of them—to tell us all what to do, how not to mess up, and how to survive while we keep their (our) beloved little hearts alive and thriving as well.

But all the advice books in the world can't really explain or even reflect that deep, primal mixture of terror and hopeless love that signifies the first months and years of parenthood. There's no advice for this condition, after all. It resists easy answers. It is insane and wonderful. It just is. When you're in the middle of it, you need more than advice. You need *stories*: stories from people who have been there, who have survived it, who are forever changed, as you are.

It's hard to describe the drama of early parenthood without sounding like a well-worn cliché. Fortunately, the talented writers featured in this collection rise to the challenge with aplomb, scaling the heights and plumbing the depths of those surreal early months and years.

Looking at these essays as a whole, you can see a consistent theme of loss: loss of identity, of freedom, of time. This is the shock of early parenthood. Who thinks about everything they've lost in becoming a parent until they're in the middle of their new lives, examining the wreckage, wondering what happened to all they once knew? Elizabeth Jarrett Andrew writes in her essay "Another Mother," "I roll out of bed and trip through the dark, abandoning all I've been for the sake of this bare need."

Parents often find themselves forced to give up their expectations. In "The Shell of Your Ear" and "States of Permanence and Impermanence," two mothers face their babies' physical challenges—hearing loss and torticollis, respectively—with grace and humor; in "Hungry," Amy Amoroso recounts her painful struggle with insufficient milk supply. Our babies, and our own bodies, can often surprise us. As Leah Laben writes in "Just Colic":

> I no longer believe all the books and authorities
> with their One True Method of Parenting that will
> yield up the child of your dreams. The child of your
> dreams is just that. The child that you actually get is
> likely to be as complicated, messy, and frustrating
> as any other human being on the planet.

Let's face it: the days after becoming a mother can be kind of anticlimactic. All that work, all that *buildup*, and all you're left with is a (temporarily) wrecked body, a yelling baby whose yelling is impossible to decipher, and (if you're lucky) a freezer full of lasagna. It's no wonder new parents can feel let down—and feel guilty for feeling let down. *How can I be sad when I have all this?* "I had a newborn in the crook of my arm and a husband in the next room, and I felt alone in the universe," Anastasia Rubis writes in "Blue Pools"—echoing, I am sure, the thoughts of new parents everywhere.

But it's not all a huge bummer. There's a lot to laugh at throughout the entire process. Take birthing class, where you might find yourself, as Eden M. Kennedy did, surrounded by young, fresh-faced hippies, all of whom are probably judging you:

> I'd brought some strawberries to share that night, and now they sat wetly in their bowl.
> "Are these organic?" asked a pale farm wife, picking up a berry and examining it.
> "No," I said. She took the berry she'd chosen and folded it into a napkin.
> Meanwhile, Farm Wife's hirsute husband was bragging to the banker couple. "We are purposely going to put the baby's bassinet on *my* side of the bed, so that when it wakes up for feeding at night, *I* have to wake up and pass the baby to my wife, so that *I'm fully participating*."

If you can't laugh through sleep deprivation, when *can* you laugh? In "The Eleven-Minute Crib Nap," Jill Christman writes of the weird power struggles that can occur between parent and baby, one of whom just wants a few minutes to get some work done: "If suckling at a mother's breast can be disgruntled, that's how Ella nursed now, her one exposed eye wide open and glaring. She wanted me to know she had my number."

But even if we lose something, becoming parents, look how much we gain! Like, say, a baby. "Babies are such a nice way to start people," the humorist Don Herold once said. In "Skin Time," Becki Melchione recalls the moment she meets one of her twins, the other still on her way via a surrogate, mere feet from her:

> I hold my hand above her face to shield her
> eyes from the bright light, and she opens them
> just enough to see my face smiling at her. I'm a
> stranger. My voice isn't the one she's heard for the
> last nine months in utero, so I introduce myself.
> "Hello, I'm Mom," I whisper, barely able to get the
> words out, "I've been waiting for you."

In "Boothville" Lisa Southgate has just given birth to the baby she's planning to give up for adoption: "The unexpected weight of him. His realness, his completeness, his well-drawn limbs, his mashed brown hair and sleepy blue eyes. He looks around the room and back at me with a heavy, skeptical gaze." I won't spoil the story by telling you how it ends.

Even if you're like Amy Penne, author of "Apocalypse Now" (the essay, not the movie), who does not think much of babies, keep in mind that babies grow up to be "smart-ass kids who talk, memorize the track listing to *Led Zeppelin IV* by age three, learn piano, collect football cards, make heart models in sixth grade, and finally learn how not to trump their partners in euchre." They're pretty cool, in other words. They can even become your role models. "He may have been small," Steven Church writes of his son ("Four Early Lessons in Parenting"), "but he thought big and wild and in ways I aspired to match."

And sometimes our new identities as parents can save us, perhaps even literally. In "Becoming His Mother," Mary A.

Scherf tells how the ordeals she faced during the adoption process helped cement her desire to be a mother, despite the damage her abusive parents had inflicted. Terrance Flynn writes in "Baby Card" of the hours before his heart transplant. Waiting to receive the new heart that will save him, he's keenly aware of the risks ahead and wants his surgeon to know that he is important, that he matters, because there's a little girl who needs him. "Tell the surgeon I'm a dad," he begs his nurse, before being wheeled into surgery.

There's so much in this collection that it's hard to encapsulate all the themes in one introduction. There are birth stories, both joyous and ambivalent; stories of adoption and surrogacy; of fertility treatments and postpartum depression; of struggling with parenthood in the wake of loss and divorce. These are twenty-three essays to be savored, whether you're up at three in the morning for another feeding, or finding yourself with a precious eleven minutes before the next nap is over. Not that you have to be a new parent to read and enjoy these glorious, heartbreaking stories—they remind all of us that life is precious, and weird, and gross, and beautifully messy. Enjoy.

And for God's sake, if the baby is sleeping, you should be, too. Go to bed.

Editor's Note

Lee Gutkind

This book has been a pleasure to edit, not just because these twenty-three true stories are so clean and well written but also because they are pleasurable, hopeful, and in most cases downright cheerful.

I suppose one might expect that from a collection of stories about babies, but *cheerful* has, unfortunately, not typically described my experience while writing about children in three books focusing on child welfare and healthcare.

Most of the true stories I have written about babies and children take place in hospitals, group homes, and psychiatric institutions, and the stories are not cute and pretty—in fact, just the opposite. (Don't get me wrong: many of my stories have positive endings; they're just not cute.) Kids at the edge of death endure heart and liver transplants—and much worse—before recovering to lead long, active lives. Infants with potentially fatal pulmonary problems lie tangled in tubes in the neonatal intensive care unit, then are cured—saved!—and on their ways home. Frightened toddlers with asthma attacks, broken arms, cuts and bruises—their panicked parents pacing the emergency room—are treated and released with smiley-face stickers on their cheeks and arms. These are nice stories, in their way. Satisfying. But even when the results are positive, kids in pain, with cancer or heart disease—or victims of abuse, neglect, and post-traumatic stress disorder—break your heart. And their survival is so very important. Babies and children are the most vital of our natural resources—the future of our nation.

How tragic, then, that we as a society are failing our infants and children and the families who support them. According to a 2013 report issued by the Children's Defense Fund, "Ending Child Poverty Now," the United States has the second-highest child poverty rate among thirty-five industrialized countries—despite having the largest economy in the world. These grim statistics have a lot to do with our elected officials. Kids and babies don't vote, after all, and young parents don't often have a lot of time or resources to devote to political campaigns. Even though politicians pay lip service to children's health and welfare, there's considerably more rhetoric than results.

Doctors, like politicians, seem to love babies and children and endorse family support systems and interactions. Yet pediatricians are on the lower rungs of the medical profession, paid far less well than physicians whose patients are primarily adults. There is a dearth of child and adolescent psychiatrists—who are paid, on average, even less than pediatricians. The American Academy of Child Psychiatry estimates that there are seven thousand child psychiatrists practicing in the United States today. In seven years, we will need thirteen thousand—but only a little more than eight thousand will be available. Child, adolescent, and young-adult mental illness is the subject of my latest book project, and a lot of the research and inter-viewing I am doing now is more than a little depressing.

So, reading all of the true stories submitted to us for con-sideration for this book and selecting those twenty-three best pieces to publish has been satisfying and, as I say, quite pleasur-able—and fun. For me, these stories have opened the door to another side of the world of babies—a positive, rewarding, joyful side that I sometimes lose in the fervor of my research. The "glorious, heartbreaking stories" in this collection, my coeditor Alice Bradley writes in her introduction, "remind all of us that life is precious, and weird, and gross, and beautifully messy."

I hope that the drama, the suspense, the tension, the sheer "gloriousness" of these pieces—not to mention the messiness—will be a reminder to all of us. We need to support our precious children in every possible way—with funding, tenderness, respect, and love. It is what they deserve.

Acknowledgments

Any book is the work of many people. The editors would especially like to thank Matt Spindler and Stephanie Bane for their careful attention to the nearly six hundred submissions we received for this project; Landon Houle for her editorial skill; Sarah Grey and Chad Vogler for copyediting; Ellen Ayoob for proofreading and project management; and the entire staff at *Creative Nonfiction* and In Fact Books.

Additionally, the Creative Nonfiction Foundation would like to express gratitude to the Juliet Lea Hillman Simonds Foundation, whose ongoing support has been essential to our success.

Schrödinger's Pregnancy

Barbara Duffey

As per usual over the last eight months, I'm naked from the waist down. I'm lying on the exam table in the same room where I found out we couldn't do in vitro fertilization (IVF). Instead, we've done an intrauterine insemination (IUI). What's the difference? With IVF, at least in our case, an embryologist performing intracytoplasmic sperm injection in a lab would use a microscopic glass needle to puncture the egg, placing the sperm inside it. With IUI, my eggs will stay in my body and, if they are fertilized, my husband's sperm will burrow through my ovum's jelly coat to fertilize the egg under its own power.

My husband pets my head. The lights are off. I try to believe that I am pregnant. I breathe deeply to improve blood flow to the uterus. We wait for the nurse practitioner to come back and tell us what to do next, when to take the pregnancy test, when it could be truly positive.

Thirty-six hours ago, I gave myself a shot of the human pregnancy hormone, human chorionic gonadotropin, or hCG, to trigger ovulation. If I take a test now, it will be positive, but that would be "trigger-shot positive," not "pregnancy positive," as Kim the nurse tells us. Observing my pregnancy is currently impossible—I am both pregnant and not-pregnant at the same time. I'm pregnant in the sense that I appear pregnant in the only way I can measure, but I'm not pregnant in that even if sperm and egg have joined, the embryo would not yet be implanted in my uterus. The pregnancy, if it exists at all, would be too new to observe.

In ancient Egypt, around 1350 BCE, women trying to find out whether they were pregnant would urinate on a barley seed and a wheat seed. If the barley grew, it was said, the woman was pregnant with a boy; if the wheat grew, a girl; if neither, she wasn't pregnant at all. When this method was tested for accuracy in the 1960s, pregnant women's urine sprouted the seeds 70 percent of the time; nonpregnant women's and men's did not. (The ability to test for gender, however, has not been confirmed.)

The home pregnancy test as we currently know it, first marketed under the brand name e.p.t. (for "Early Pregnancy Test," then "Error-Proof Test"), was approved by the FDA in 1976 and sold for the first time in 1977, according to the National Institutes of Health. In 1978, its manufacturer, Warner Chilcott, advertised the new product in women's magazines such as *Mademoiselle, Ladies' Home Journal, Good Housekeeping*, and *Vogue*. *Mademoiselle* described the contents in a 1978 article: "For your $10, you get pre-measured ingredients consisting of a vial of purified water, a test tube containing, among other things, sheep red blood cells . . . as well as a medicine dropper and clear plastic support for the test tube, with an angled mirror at the bottom."

After the insemination, my mother takes my husband and me to the aquarium, which used to be a Toys"R"Us. It's a five-minute drive from the fertility clinic, and my husband has been dying to see the penguins. I pay our admission fee and we head straight for the exhibit; they were fed an hour ago, so now they're active and loud. Two penguins in the corner have their backs to us and their heads together, plotting. Another penguin sits on the fake rock next to the water, throat-singing. Several penguins jump into and out of the water; one floats next to the glass, centimeters from our faces, looking at us first from above, then below the water, then above, then below again. This penguin treads water on its belly and conducts its optics experiment over and over again. A little girl yells, "Penguins!"

"Oh, yes!" my husband says. "That's exactly how I feel."

I thought it would be hard seeing the children at the aquarium, since each one seemed a screaming reminder of what I couldn't do and couldn't have, but today I'm hopeful. I feel I can will my own children to happen. We visit the sea-horse and sea dragon exhibit; my husband stands under a sign that reads, "Seahorses: Super Dad!" I feel crampy, as if it were the first day of my period. I try to believe this means the IUI worked, though I know any zygote would only be a fertilized egg floating in my fallopian tube. A female seahorse lays her eggs outside of her body, into the egg pouch of the male; the male then fertilizes them and carries the eggs until they hatch. While seahorses have a special pouch to carry the eggs, in the closely related sea dragon species, males carry the fertilized eggs on their tails. Reading a sign with the heading "Long Odds," we learn that "out of the 250 eggs the female sea dragon may lay on the tail of the male, only 5 percent may reach maturity." I wish I had 5 percent odds, that 5 percent of all my eggs were good; if this egg in my follicle is good, I have what my doctor called "as good a chance as anyone else for the IUI: 20 percent"—but that's a pretty big *if*. I realize the sea dragon's "long odds" assume an egg's point of view: that is, each egg finds it hard to survive. But the mother will most likely reproduce; I envy her certainty.

The reason it took so long to develop an accurate pregnancy test is that scientists had trouble isolating hCG from other hormones associated with female fertility, particularly luteinizing hormone (LH) and follicle-stimulating hormone (FSH). In 1927, German gynecologists Selmar Aschheim and Bernhard Zondek invented a process that came to be known as the A-Z test. They injected the urine of a possibly pregnant woman into an immature rat. If the woman wasn't pregnant, the rat would not react. But if she was pregnant, the rat would go into heat, even though it was immature. They theorized that women produced an increased amount of a substance during pregnancy (they called it "prolan") that triggered the estrous reaction in rats. In the 1930s, scientists injected this substance, which since 1950 has been called hCG, into rabbits, frogs, toads, and rats to induce ovulation, just as in 2011 hCG induced ovulation in me. This process was soon used to diagnose pregnancy: A woman's urine would be injected into an animal and, after a week or so, the animal would be cut open to see whether her ovaries had developed. These tests were slow, required extensive animal sacrifice, and often gave false positives because they weren't sensitive enough to tell the difference between hCG and LH, which a woman produces when she ovulates. Scientists in the 1960s instead turned to radioimmunoassays, the use of radioactive substances to detect antibodies to certain hormones in order to deduce the presence of those hormones.

They, too, came up against the problem of distinguishing hCG from LH. But in 1972, Judith Vaitukaitis, Glenn Braunstein, and Griff Ross, American researchers at the National Institutes of Health, published a paper identifying a subunit of hCG, the beta-subunit, that is immunologically and biologically different from LH and, therefore, makes a case for itself as what to look for in pregnancy tests. This is what e.p.t. and subsequent at-home pregnancy tests check for; the test strip is coated with proteins that react to the beta-subunit of hCG present in a pregnant woman's urine.

I can't escape the feeling that I'm no longer an animal, that my infertility has rendered me only a mind. My body, with its "diminished ovarian reserve," cannot function as bodies are meant to function, as creative spaces for the perpetuation and mutation of a species. Mine just seems like a vehicle to move my brain in front of stimuli, stimuli that should spark a creative response and thus a creative output that could stand in for my lack of ability to actually create another human being, my creativity thus forever metaphoric. *Here, let me tell you about the seahorses, the sea dragons, the jellyfish, because I have no baby to show you.*

The jellyfish have their own nook at the aquarium. Inside the nook are three tanks: one for the moon jellyfish, one for the sea nettles, and one for the upside-down jellyfish. Sea nettles can release forty thousand eggs a day, at least some of which unite with sperm that have been released into the water by another jellyfish. Fertilized eggs become larvae, which attach to hard surfaces, become polyps, and then elongate and bud off to release many young jellyfish. Several polyps together can produce tens of thousands of jellyfish at once.

All I want is one. I don't need tens of thousands of babies. Just the one—and that feels impossible.

In the 1990s, pregnancy tests began using enzyme markers instead of radioactive markers to distinguish hCG from LH. In 2003, Clearblue Easy released a digital-readout pregnancy test that displays the words "Pregnant" or "Not Pregnant" instead of a colored line. I took my first pregnancy test before 2003, but I never doubted that language would stand in for my fertility—you would think the line so clearly and immediately communicates its signified, that letters would feel redundant, indulgent, baroque. This signified would be the feeling "happy" or "not happy," though the signifier corresponding to "happy" or "not happy" would differ from person to person, and many people would feel not one or the other but both at once. I want those letters, the clarity of them, someone speaking to me— even if the someone is a stick I peed on.

The day after the IUI, I administer my first progesterone vaginal insert. Progesterone, as the name implies, promotes gestation—it helps the uterine lining grow. If I'm to have a baby, not only must the egg be fertilized but the resulting embryo must also implant itself in my uterus. My mother drives me to school; I begin to feel nauseated. It will be the first of many pregnancy symptoms I'll experience over the next week: I'll fall asleep at seven in the evening watching a soccer match on TV, I'll feel insatiable for no reason and eat more than I should, I'll have gas and think it's some kind of cramp. I know of no corollary to this, the feeling that the most important thing in my life might be happening and there's no way I can find out if it is or if it isn't. There are no indicators at all. A fertilized egg would be untethered, moving inside me, unable to provide feedback to my body and yet contained by my body. I cannot imagine how embryos don't just fall out of the body altogether. How does the uterus ever catch them?

Many people use Schrödinger's cat—the cat in the closed box, which may be alive or dead, but you can't tell until you open the box—as an example of any lack of knowledge, this inability to know if something is happening or not. This application of the physicist's thought experiment is, however, a misrepresentation of what Erwin Schrödinger actually said. In his experiment, which was designed as an illustration of a problem in quantum mechanics, the issue isn't uncertainty about the cat being dead. Rather, the cat is *both* dead and not dead at once. The cat shares a box with a vial of poison triggered by the depletion of a radioactive isotope. If the isotope decays enough, the vial is opened and the cat dies. If the isotope remains somewhat intact, the cat is safe. The radioactive material has an equal chance of decaying or not over the course of an hour. Those who study quantum mechanics would say that there is a "superposition" of states, that after the first hour, the material exists both as decayed and as not decayed until we can view it. They use such conceptualizations to describe the probabilities their field utilizes; for example, scientists represent an electron's position probabilistically because they can't observe it directly. But if the material is both decayed and not decayed, then the vial is also opened and unopened, and the cat is both dead *and* alive. Schrödinger intended the thought experiment as a critique of quantum mechanics and its processes; the cat can't be both at once.

In response, scientists who study quantum mechanics argue that the problem lies with our understanding of reality, not with quantum mechanics—in their conception of the world, the cat *is* both dead and alive because of superposition. That is to say, when we open the box, it doesn't mean that the state of the cat is finally revealed—it means that *observing* the cat is what makes the cat either alive or dead. Before that, it was both, according to quantum mechanics. Similarly, if my egg is fertilized but not attached, I am both pregnant and not pregnant; in that way, the invocation of Schrödinger is apt. I am in that hour of possible decay. I am waiting to be observed, waiting for my chance to take a pregnancy test that will give me an accurate reading, not just a trigger-shot positive reading.

By day three, I'm no longer nauseated, but I'm still riding a strange wave of hope. I have coffee (decaf) with a friend that morning; it's snowing. I think of when my due date will be. I imagine myself as a sea nettle with thousands of offspring growing on the ocean floor, so that the whole ocean becomes my nursery and my genes are everywhere.

On day four, I'm feeling less optimistic. I'm not sure if my response is hormonal, emotional, or intellectual. I don't want to get my hopes up. I want my expectations to match the probability of my success. I should be 20 percent hopeful, I think. I think back to the prelude to the IUI; Kim the nurse had my husband's semen sample in a needle attached to a catheter. She showed it to both of us so we could confirm it was ours. The stickers on the catheter and our paperwork were color-coded yellow. She said his sample contained a million sperm. He asked if that was good. She said they like to have five million, but "it only takes one!" She said that after all we'd been through, she wasn't going to call the procedure off. At the time, I thought, *it only takes one*. Now, on day four, I think, *this was a cancelable IUI and we did it anyway*. Who was I to think it would work? Perhaps I should be 4 percent hopeful.

On day five, I see my dissertation director and explain the differences between IVF and IUI, that my eggs are released into my body and inseminated just as in "normal" people. She asks about odds and success rates. I give the optimistic number, the number that assumes my egg was good and, I guess, that my husband had five million sperm in his sample. She tries to think back to the first two weeks of her first pregnancy, but she can't remember any noticeable signs. I say that there are no signs, that even if the egg were fertilized, it wouldn't have implanted and thus couldn't give feedback to my body. She says she'll say my name in synagogue. I thank her.

On day six, I go to my infertility support group. I show up two minutes late and all the other ladies are already there. The hostess says they've been talking about me. I'd run into another member, Michelle, at the fertility clinic—it is one of only two in town—on the day I'd had the ultrasound that showed only one of my follicles had grown enough to mature an egg, and she's probably told them my news. Women who do successful IVF procedures have ten or twenty mature follicles, as compared to my one, and women with polycystic ovarian syndrome can have fifty. They can hyperstimulate. The blood vessels in their ovaries react to the hCG too much, and the ovaries swell and sometimes leak fluid into the abdomen. Hyperstimulation can even lead to death; it's rare, but it does happen. The women at the support group have never *not* stimulated, but they have hyperstimulated, and the result is often the same—no baby.

Finally, on day ten, I go to the twenty-four-hour Walgreens at midnight after my friend's birthday party, at which I sat around trying to be clever without having anything to drink. "I brought the Martinelli's," I said. "Time to get this party started!" It did not go well. My friend was dressed in sequins and laughed at my jokes, probably out of pity, but the other women looked at me uncomfortably, unsure what they should do or say. They offered me things I couldn't eat, unpasteurized goat cheese and charcuterie. They wanted to talk about new crushes and who was dating whom and who had gotten what job at what publication, and it was hard to include me in any discussion. I wasn't helping, either; when they would look at me for confirmation that they were including me and that their topics were okay with me, I would realize that I was staring off into space or petting the cat too much. I would respond by telling bad jokes. It was hard to tell if my brain made better jokes when I'd had something to drink or if I told the jokes with more aplomb because the alcohol helped me believe in them more. Around eleven-thirty, I realized all I had been doing was fantasizing about buying a pregnancy test. So here I am at Walgreens.

I decide I'll get the Clearblue Easy digital kind; why not take advantage of one of the only advances in pregnancy-test technology since the seventies? The digital versions are much more expensive than the others, but I decide my sanity is worth it—I don't want to decipher the darkness of a line or the length of the bump of color perpendicular to the test line. I just want it to tell me. In language. "Pregnant" or "Not Pregnant." I also buy two bottles of Perrier and a *Vogue* magazine. I wonder if I'm trying to hide the test, make it look like it's just

one of many things I'm buying so the cashier won't notice. It
turns out he's on the phone with someone who needs a type
of contact-lens solution they don't carry; he and his manager
are arguing about where the customer could get that kind of
solution at midnight on a Saturday, and he rings me up without even looking at what I'm buying, which is a relief. This
moment is too big and intimate to share with him, but he must
be used to that, ringing up the proof of what goes on inside
everyone else's bodies, the pregnancy tests, the antidiarrheals,
the laxatives. Health must always seem contingent and fleeting
to him. Or not; everyone else's is contingent and fleeting, his a
monolith of youth and vigor.

I come home with extra cupcakes from the party, give my
husband his Perrier, and take out the pregnancy test. We discover we have different memories of when Kim the nurse told
us to take it; I remember her saying we'd probably be fine by
the weekend, but we should wait until Tuesday to make sure.
I think we should test now and then again on Tuesday. My
husband remembers instructions not to take it on the weekend
but to wait for Tuesday. I say that I don't want my period to be
the indicator that I'm not pregnant; I want the test to tell me
"Not Pregnant" in English, to my face, like a man! I say maybe
I'll take one today and then one again on Tuesday. He agrees,
but I can tell it's the kind of agreement that means he doesn't
want to argue with me anymore. It's not the kind of agreement
that means he agrees. I suggest I take it the next morning, as
a compromise, and then again on Tuesday. He agrees to that,
and I decide that since it's close enough to what I want to do,
I'm not going to analyze what kind of agreement that might be.
It's my pee, after all.

On day eleven, I wake up first. I read *Angle of Repose* and eat Thanksgiving leftovers. When my husband gets up, he asks if I've taken the test. I say I've reconsidered; I don't want it to ruin my day. I'll take it later. We go to the pancake house for a meal, buy several paperbacks at the bookstore down the street, take the dog to the dog park. When we get home, I decide I'll take the test; there's a Scandinavian detective miniseries on TV, so if the test says "Not Pregnant," I'll drink red wine and watch Maria Wern solve murders on her island off Göteborg. It feels safe to take it now.

I can't get the cellophane off. I have to cut it with scissors. I open the box and read the instructions; it's very adamant that I should never hold the test with the test strip up; hold the test down or level only. I should urinate on the stick for five seconds. I do. I re-cap the test strip and wait. The test flashes a picture of an hourglass with the sands halfway fallen. The instructions say this means the test is working, and I have to wait three minutes for the result. I wash my hands and watch myself in the mirror; I fix my hair, even though it's in such a sloppy knot that "fixing" doesn't really do anything, until the test stops flashing and says something.

It says "Pregnant."

I take it into the living room to show my husband.

"It says 'Pregnant,'" I say.

He squeals a little in excitement. I notice hope in his eyes, a little sparkle before practical concerns return. "We shouldn't get too happy yet," he says. "When it still says 'Pregnant' on Tuesday, then we'll call them."

"I know," I say. "But this is the only thing it could say if I am pregnant."

"Right!"

"So I'm going to be happy about it for now."

"OK!" he says, and we agree to be happy.

"I guess you're not going to have a drink to celebrate," he says.

"Guess not!" I say. I try to keep reading *Angle of Repose*, but I have trouble concentrating. I feel crampy again, as I did the day of the IUI, but I don't want to think about it. I live in fear that I will get my period.

On day twelve, I wake up and still no period. I go to work but can't imagine how I'll pay attention to anything; I just want it to be Tuesday morning already.

Even years later, I cannot remember what happened in the time between that weekend and the Tuesday when I took another test.

Which also said "Pregnant."

I shook my husband awake and he yelled and the dog barked from her crate in the kitchen and the test said "Pregnant" and I called the clinic for a blood test. Which, to spare some suspense, confirmed that I was, indeed, at that moment, pregnant. Then I began the long wait for the six-week transvaginal ultrasound, after which my miscarriage risk would be 2 percent. But then, that morning, I felt fertile and floaty, like a jellyfish suspended in salt water and beautifully translucent, available to view.

Birthing Class

Eden M. Kennedy

The first time I realized that all my parenting choices would be examined and then rejected by other, smugger parents happened during birthing class. My husband and I, along with three younger couples, had staked out our spots in a soulless meeting room full of folding chairs at St. Francis Hospital in Santa Barbara. Each two-hour class took place once a week during the dinner hour, so we had to bring snacks to share. Believe me when I tell you the snack table was stacked and tended with the laser-like focus only pregnant women can have for hummus and grapes.

Two of the couples seemed already to know each other. The women were twenty-something farm-wife types who wore homemade cotton print skirts and looked like they canned their own lingonberries. Their bearded husbands greeted each other with a hearty laugh and a clap on the back. The first time this happened, Jack and I turned our heads in unison to watch this almost quaint display of masculine jocularity.

"Maybe that's how they greet each other down at the Moose Lodge," I whispered.

Jack rolled his eyes. He had spent all day on a construction site and was not happy about giving up his evening to any activity that didn't involve our couch, a beer, and the Lakers game.

The other couple was in their thirties and Latino and kept to themselves, like us. I exchanged a polite smile with them, but then they both looked away. I decided they worked in a bank, but not the same bank, both in customer service, and now that they were off work they didn't want to talk to anyone but each other. It was simpler than thinking they didn't want to talk to me.

The classes were taught by a young woman named Myrrh, a shy apprentice midwife and registered nurse who was charging each couple $150 for six classes. Jack and I were already paying three thousand dollars out of pocket for the midwives because my health insurance wouldn't cover their services. Finances were tight, so coughing up an extra $150 to be told a bunch of things I'd much rather read while standing in the pregnancy section of a local bookstore was no small intrusion on our budget—and something of an insult to my intelligence. The classes were optional and we could have quit at any time, but I rationalized the expense by telling myself that maybe I'd discover something I'd overlooked in my somewhat hit-or-miss birth preparations.

Jack remained openly resentful that the midwives had pressured us into being here. "Has it been a slow month for babies?" he said as we waited for Myrrh to queue up her PowerPoint presentation. He said it loud enough for her to hear, but she was busy looking for an outlet for her laptop. It was Jack's belief that the midwives were just trying to keep Myrrh busy while business was slow. He was probably right, but as I watched

Myrrh poke tentatively at her keyboard, I felt like a little public-speaking experience might do her some good.

The first class covered breathing and relaxation techniques. Since I'd been doing yoga for five years, I listened with the sort of condescension that you often find in yoga students who think they know a lot more than they really do. Myrrh outlined the Lamaze method for us. It seemed impossible that chanting *hoo-hoo-ha-ha* at precisely timed intervals was still being promoted as a state-of-the-art technique; it seemed so outdated, so seventies. I was sure that the ancient yoga masters would have had something far wiser to say about dissolving your labor pains, if only they weren't dead. I looked over at Jack. He had dropped his chin to his chest and was pretending to nod off to sleep. Then he jerked up with an entertaining little snort. I elbowed him and whispered, "*Stop it!*" I hoped that Myrrh hadn't seen him.

Despite this rather unpromising start, I was determined to get my full $150 worth of lecturing, so on we marched to the next class. The second session was about coaching and how our partners could support us during birth, which seemed to center on pushing a tennis ball into my lower back. Myrrh handed out a single tennis ball for us to pass around. She got the men to practice pushing it into different points on their partners' backs. They were supposed to search for the spots that felt best to the women. Since I wasn't actually in labor, it was hard to know what to ask Jack to do, but the technique seemed promising in that it would give Jack something to do during birth besides sit there and stare at me. (Of course, seven weeks later, when I went into labor and Jack tried to hold my hand during a contraction, I politely told him to get the hell away from me.

I then went to bed and spent the next several hours alone in the dark, mooing like a cow while he read a magazine in the living room. If I'd had a tennis ball then, I probably would have chewed on it.)

After the coaching session, we learned about what to expect postpartum. It was common, Myrrh said, to pass large blood clots after the baby was born, and the series of frustrated sighs that came from my immediate right reminded me that my husband had zero interest in doctors, medical terminology, or esoteric bodily functions, normal or otherwise. Still, I tried to focus on Myrrh's instruction. She was encouraging us women to think about how we were going to let ourselves be taken care of after the birth; though this sounds simple in theory—*Let your partner worry about the grocery shopping! He can make you a sandwich if you're too busy nursing to make lunch!*—it would turn out to be one of the most psychologically difficult parts of the whole birth process for me. I discovered that my lifelong independent streak ran parallel to a more troubling notion that if I didn't do for myself, no one else would bother because I wasn't worth the trouble.

That would have been a rational way to continue to function had I been alone, but I was a married woman whose husband, despite his reluctance in birthing class, was surprisingly thoughtful. He cooked dinner every night and cheerfully went out and bought two boxes of maxi pads when I finally broke down and asked. That simple request took me to a level of humility and surrender for which all Myrrh's best efforts could never have fully prepared me.

The birthing sessions continued. I discovered taking a class about breastfeeding was like taking a class about having sex. Afterward, you think you have a handle on what's going to go where, but when you finally get your shirt off, it turns out the other person has completely different expectations. Myrrh emphasized something called the "football hold" which, when I finally tried it on my own baby, resulted in a lot of confusion and crying, mostly on my part. Jack was helpless to do anything but watch as a brusque lactation consultant named Kitty strolled into our apartment and flipped our surprised baby around into different positions until we found one that worked. Nonetheless, he did his part by listening to me squawk as the baby latched onto my sore, swollen boob. He left the house and came back, quietly handing me a jar of nipple balm.

On the night Myrrh was scheduled to talk about the labor process, medical procedures, and hospital transfers for a C-section in case something went awry with our home birthing plans, Jack had had enough. "I'm not going," he said, sunburned and covered in sawdust. He pried the cap off a Corona. "I had a day from hell, and I hate hospitals. I don't want to think about you ending up in one."

It didn't seem like the greatest excuse, given that we had been going to a hospital every week to take these classes—"It's not the same thing," Jack said—but I had no wish to argue. I am by nature an introvert, and though I really didn't want to go to class without having him to hide behind, I felt like I'd get in trouble somehow if I didn't go, or poor Myrrh would feel bad, or this would turn out to be the one class that was vital to my birth experience. In the end, going alone was easier than making some sort of fuss I didn't even know how to make in order to get Jack to do something he really didn't want to do.

When I arrived alone at the hospital meeting room, the heartiest back-clapper of the two bearded husbands, the Beard, came over and asked me where Jack was. Unprepared to tell a flattering lie about my husband working late, I simply told him what Jack had said: "He hates hospitals." It seemed stupid with us all standing in a hospital meeting room, so then I said the thing that felt truer: "And he doesn't want to have to think about what might happen if something goes wrong for me or the baby."

This wasn't something we'd ever talked about in any detail. Jack was a classic strong, silent type who didn't go on and on about his feelings but would dissolve into great gulping sobs when Merle Oberon's Cathy died at the end of *Wuthering Heights*. I knew he loved me and cared about our child's safe entrance into our rented plastic birthing tub, but to entertain even the slightest possibility that childbirth could kill me or our baby was not something he wanted to face in a roomful of hairy home-birthers.

This admission, made with unusual vulnerability on my part, was met with frank and open derision by the Beard. Initially, Jack's presence had stunned the other, younger fathers into beta status. Being tall and tough-talking, Jack often comes off as one of the most alpha of alpha males. Once he had removed himself from the pack, though, the betas clearly had a lot to say about what they now perceived as his weakness.

The Beard shook his head in pity for me. "So, what, he'd make you go to the hospital by yourself if you needed a C-section?"

The other hairy husband crossed his arms and said, "Lame."

The bankers exchanged a look but said nothing.

Apparently, Jack not showing up had pressed a button, and that button opened a hatch, and out of that hatch flew all the self-satisfaction they'd been suppressing. I'd been having some superior feelings of my own, of course, but it was unnerving to have theirs out in the open and aimed at me.

Then Myrrh dimmed the lights and the video about C-sections began, and the hairy men put their arms protectively around their womenfolk. I sat alone, heavy against the hard metal chair. The Head Beard gave me one last look, a lasting glance that said these men were not afraid of hospitals, and I was on my own.

The video was terrible. Not terrible in the sense of bad; it was an old but well-produced half-hour television documentary about one woman's black-and-white journey from hospital admission to operating room to recovery room to, finally, an adjustable bed where she nursed her brand-new, safe, healthy baby. No, it was terrible in the sense that it inspired terror in me. I didn't want to be pushed down a bright hallway on a gurney with a paper cap on my head and no one to hold my hand because my hospital-hating husband had dropped me off at the emergency room and gone home to watch the game and drink beer and wait for me to call when it was over. How dare he abandon me like that! Like this! I fought back tears for the entire half hour. When the lights came back on, I waddled to the snack table to blow my nose on a cocktail napkin. I'd brought some strawberries to share that night, and now they sat wetly in their bowl.

"Are these organic?" asked a pale farm wife, picking up a berry and examining it.

"No," I said. She took the berry she'd chosen and folded it into a napkin.

Meanwhile, Farm Wife's hirsute husband was bragging to the banker couple. "We are purposely going to put the baby's bassinet on *my* side of the bed, so that when it wakes up for feeding at night, *I* have to wake up and pass the baby to my wife, so that *I'm fully participating*."

The bankers glanced at me with an expression of what I wanted to think was veiled sympathy. This guy, I thought, was trying a little too hard to prove what a great dad he was going to be. I knew then that if I had to choose between a husband who skipped a pregnancy class but made dinner for me every night and a guy who could not foresee the necessity of at least one parent getting a full night's sleep, I'd married the right guy after all.

That night, over Jack's chicken piccata, I talked all about the horrible movie and the hairy man's weird declaration. Jack hugged me and thanked me for letting him off the hook. He promised that he wouldn't miss the last one (when Myrrh would bring out a stuffed fabric pelvis and we'd watch her awkwardly push a plastic baby doll through it, head first) and that he'd never abandon me in the ER parking lot. He said the Beard was crazy and dumb and unimportant and that, once this was over, we'd never have to see him again. We had good help, we knew what we were doing, and everything would be okay.

Indeed, it was okay, as luck would have it; I appreciated our fortune even more after learning about all the ways the whole thing could have gone wrong. My son's birth went swiftly and safely. I didn't end up alone in a hospital, crying in a paper hat. Jack continues to be unaffected by the judgments of people who don't matter to him. He was wrong about one thing, though:

we did see the Beard and Farm Wife a couple of years later. They were coming out of the midwife's office and getting into a Volkswagen Bug. Farm Wife wore a kerchief tied sweetly around her head; she was pregnant again. The Beard still had his beard. They both looked pretty happy, and I thought, *probably so do we.*

Push

Wanda Pitschel Harding

At midnight on my due date, my water breaks while I'm in bed. My husband can't get his mind around this really happening and insists it is sweat or maybe pee or something, anything else. He remembers from birthing class that amniotic fluid is sweet. So we tentatively smell the dark spot on our sheets. Now I am wondering if I actually did pee; your body takes over when you're pregnant, and you don't always know what's going on or when. You're just the passenger along for the ride. Barry can't smell anything. He gingerly taps the wetness with his index finger, then touches his lips.

"Oh my God," he says. "Your water broke."

Fourteen hours later, I'm wondering if a person can stay alive in such pain. Doesn't pain signal bad things, like paralyzing injury or death? Birthing class used words like *pressure*, *discomfort*, *opening*. Now these terms seem like cruel lies.

My husband and I decided to have a child late in life. In fact, *decided* is too strong a word. I spent a year interviewing my sisters and my friends with children, trying to determine why people undertake such a daunting responsibility. Married thirteen years, my husband and I had learned to take love past infatuation and convenience to true acceptance. The joy and strength we experienced from our changing relationship caused us to think that maybe we could love a child. Maybe it would be deep and beautiful and profound. Maybe. I was thirty-nine. If pregnant, I would be medically defined as at an "advanced maternal age." We discussed ourselves into circles—and then the decision was made for us. As many a knocked-up sixteen-year-old knows, it only takes once.

So here we are, middle-aged and about to give birth, as nervous and ambivalent about becoming parents as the above-mentioned teenagers.

At four in the morning, I insist we call Ann, our midwife. Barry wants me to wait until six. I am sure she said to call if the water breaks. He is sure she said it can be a long time after the water breaks, so don't call then, but wait until you can't talk during a contraction. I can't believe this is correct and remind him that Ann is usually up at four, training for the marathon, so we won't wake her if we do call. Barry says she doesn't train that early *every* day.

Turns out he was right on both counts. A weary Ann tells me she was up until two delivering a baby, and says to call back when I can't talk during a contraction. That still seems way too late in the process to me.

We wait as long as I can stand it, until around nine. Ann asks Barry to hold the phone up to me. When she hears my forceful breathing, she agrees it's time. She and her young assistant, Laurie, arrive at our house thirty minutes later.

Ann has more than thirty years of experience. She's an
RN, a marathoner, and a local celebrity among the granola
set. Originally, I had seen a traditional OB/GYN. Waiting
an hour for a ten-minute office visit was typical, and when
I finally saw the doctor, I often felt less reassured and more
abnormal. She always recommended more tests because
of my age. I was thirty-nine, not ninety-nine! My mother
had had me at thirty-nine and my younger brother four
years later. Still, I tried to make it work with the OB/GYN.
I explained that I wanted the baby handed to me right after
birth so I could immediately begin nursing. I didn't want
a hospital worker to take the baby for washing and tests.
But none of my desires concerned the doctor. All she cared
about, she said, was delivering a healthy baby. Nothing else
mattered. She couldn't seem to understand that I wanted a
healthy baby *and* for my child to have a gentle introduction to
this world. She couldn't even guarantee she would be present
at the delivery. There was a fifty-fifty chance I would get her
partner, who was even more dispassionate.

After this discussion, I went to visit Ann. The first time she
saw me, she lightly stroked the two-thirds globe attached to
my torso and said, "Isn't it beautiful? Isn't it amazing?" Right
then, I signed up for the road less traveled. I felt Ann's enthu-
siasm could help me with my mixed feelings about becoming
a mother, which was not a small or unimportant feat. A little
extra bonding with the baby at the outset couldn't hurt either.

I try many positions. What seemed logical in birthing
class—*let gravity help*—now disappoints. Where is the focus

I'd read about, the calm during labor? Each time I find a bit of relief on the sofa or big exercise ball, I think, *There, now I can handle this. Let me go deeper into this place and everything will be okay.* But to Ann, I am "slowing down," and that is a bad thing. She has transformed into a medieval torturer. "Keep walking," she commands. This is painful but bearable. "Climb the stairs," she says. Excruciating and very near impossible. I have to pause on each stair to brace myself for the next one. But I am obedient. I am silent. I am in my own little world of suffering. I wonder how torture victims survive. I know this will end with a baby. I know it will take somewhere between two and twenty-four hours. I remind myself this is *natural* pain.

I cling to my husband like a life raft, so hard that the next day he has five fingerprint bruises on his forearm. We walk around the den, past the French doors opening onto the leafy backyard, through the dining room, up the stairs, tight circle on the landing, past the baby's room, and down again. No time to linger in my new favorite room, which Barry painted twice to get the right shade of ballerina pink (the first was too Pepto-Bismol). Ann wants me moving, preferably on stairs. No peeking inside the new cream-colored armoire, as I've done many times in the last few months, to adjust the pastel piles of tiny onesies, washed, folded, and waiting like rolls of Smarties candies. Behind my veil of pain, I barely notice the room. Up and down, up and down. Hour after hour. The birthing assistant follows us with the vomit bucket.

Every so often, Ann stops me. She places her handheld Doppler on my big, hard belly. She listens to the baby's heartbeat, the strong hummingbird percussion.

Ann wonders why this is taking so long. She checks me and says a bit of cervix is stuck, and asks if she can move it to "help things along." *Yes, yes.* I lie on the sofa and Barry kneels on the floor, holding my hand. She is right to warn that it "might hurt." This might not be a big deal when one isn't in the middle of labor, but at this point, everything below my Stretch Armstrong belly button is tender and swollen and defensive. I gasp. These millimeter nudges are jarring, like popping a dislocated shoulder back in place.

We do the up-and-down-loop parade many more times. The concept of time is gone for me, except to think, *Surely it has been enough. Surely the baby will be born soon.*

Barry makes me a "birthing smoothie," a recipe from Ann. They urge me to take a sip to help me stay strong. The veil of pain has formed itself into a cocoon. They offer the smoothie several times before they get through to me. I am not interested in food or water, but I take a sip, partly to get them to leave me alone about the smoothie and partly because I am deferring to the hired expert.

Generally, when a baby is far enough down the birth canal, the woman feels the urge to push. This is often one of the benefits of not having an epidural—you can feel when it is time, which allows you to push with the contractions for maximum effectiveness. But I am not feeling the urge. So we keep going: up and down, up and down. Laurie and Ann take turns eating lunches brought from home. Laurie puts the pink baby blankets in the oven on warm. I am still not feeling ready to push.

Ann checks the heartbeat again. This time, she can't hear it. She tries again and again, with me in several different positions. Each time I hold my breath, sure she will hear the hummingbird thrumming. Nothing.

Ann says, "It's probably fine." Most likely, she explains, the baby is just turned away from us. "But you need to get it out now," she says, "to be sure."

I can't allow myself to be afraid. There isn't time, and everything depends on me. I trust Ann and her calm professionalism. I am sure I can push this baby out quickly and safely. I am fit. I am motivated. Pushing, here we go. I bear down for one big strain, then . . . burning, searing pain. I stop immediately. It feels as if my vital female parts are being torn in two. Not pressure, not tingling, certainly not relief like some of the books said about pushing; more like being drawn and quartered. *I can't do this,* I think. *It's suicide.*

Ann must have seen this scenario before because—without my saying a word—she says, "It's okay. You're not damaging anything. This is how it feels to have a baby."

I am silent, appreciating the reassurance. But is she sure? She doesn't know what I feel inside. I trust Ann, but of course I know that women used to die in childbirth. Natural childbirth proponents explain that most of that was due to blood loss or infection afterward. But what if I am the exception? I put the thought away because I know it is probably fine and, anyway, what am I going to do about it at this point? I can't think. I've got to push.

It's hard to push using unfamiliar muscles. There is no training for it. I take a guess and squeeze the muscles of my lower abdomen, but nothing happens. "Don't breathe out with it like when you lift weights," Ann tells me. "Hold your breath and push hard like you're having a stubborn bowel movement." I try many more times. I try different positions. I end up on my back on the big plastic sheet Laurie has spread on the den carpet. Ann puts her hand inside me until she can feel the baby's head and tells me to push. "That didn't do anything—try again, a little differently." I try a few variations. It's like trying to make music on an instrument you've never played before. Then, finally, "That's it. That moved her a bit. Keep going."

I push and push. "Grunt when you bear down. It helps. You don't have to be silent," Ann says. "It's okay to yell and scream and swear." I don't want to do any of those things. I grunt only because she says it helps.

Ann puts the Doppler on my big, bare belly again. Still no heartbeat. "You've got to get this baby out *now*." Ann's normal gentleness is edged with stern determination. Barry is at my side. He is quiet, as usual, which is just what I need now. He tells me later that he wasn't scared. Maybe it was ignorance, he says, but he had an otherworldly assurance that everything would be okay. Maybe I sense this, I don't know—but I do know that his quiet strength allows me to focus on the task at hand.

Once we are in this desperate place, after a few searing pushes, I no longer register pain. I am a woman with a baby who might die if I don't get it out. I can feel the baby retreat a millimeter or two after every millimeter forward. It feels like a Sisyphean task: up the pelvic hill, then back down. The pushing seems almost useless, but I do it with everything I've got. I don't wail or think *I can't do this*. There is only one thing to do and that is PUSH. So I push.

I push, and push, and push.

Three people are yelling at me: "Push, push!" *Can't they see I am pushing?*

I push more, as hard and as fast as I can. It feels like hours go by. I wonder if I will push her out in time. There is no time to panic, no time to cry. There is only time to push.

Push. Push.

The baby isn't progressing enough. I don't know what else to do. I am huffing for breath. No one can push for me. We can't take turns. I am failing her. I am failing my daughter before she is even born.

Unbidden, a thought comes: *It will be okay if she dies. It will be as though the last nine months never happened. It will be safe, easy.*

I wonder if Ann sees something in my face because she tells her assistant to call the ambulance. She grabs my knees and looks at me hard. "Push this baby out before the ambulance gets here."

I grab onto this hope. *I can do this before the ambulance comes.* Thoughts of death vanish. I go back inside myself and find this: I can't play it safe. I have to push with total disregard for my body. For the baby stuck inside me, I will myself to do this. I push like a wild animal that goes off by itself and does what needs to be done. Quietly, but fiercely. Savagely. Maroon-faced and sweaty, teeth bared, fists tight as rocks.

Push, and push, and push.

"I'm going to cut an episiotomy." She's only done two in her long career. Natural tearing heals more easily, but I guess I am not tearing naturally. Months ago, sitting on a floor pillow with five other couples in Ann's birthing class, either way of opening up sounded awful. Now I don't care. There is no room in me for fear. GET THE BABY OUT has completely filled my heart, my brain, my consciousness, my ego, my womb: me. A woman cuts my nether regions with a scalpel. I'm not on any pain medicine, but I don't flinch. I don't feel a thing. I will be told later that blood squirted out six inches into the air. Barry is his stoic self, watching right next to me. Apparently unfazed, he puts his arm around me.

"You've got plenty of room now," Ann says. "Get this baby out!"

I push: she moves up the hill.

Another push: I stop her from coming back down the hill.

I push and—

"She's crowning!" Ann yells. "You can do it!"

Barry moves down to look. He later told me, "I saw a one-inch diameter circle of the top of her head and instantly felt overwhelming love for her."

He also tells me about the ambulance, which arrived along with a police car and a fire truck. All staffed. I'm lying completely naked on my den floor and suddenly there are five community helpers standing a polite six feet away. I didn't hear a knock on the door or see them walk inside. It is as if they beamed themselves here, like in *Star Trek*. I don't register that they can see my big, pregnant bare breasts or my formerly private parts between my sweaty legs. I couldn't be more exposed, but that doesn't even come into my consciousness. I am out of my body and, at the same time, I am nothing but a body.

With my birth canal cut wider and my steady rock of a husband behind me to provide counterforce, I lean in, grab the underside of my knees, and

PUSH

PUSH

"I can see the whole top of her head. She's coming!"

PUSH

PUSH

My pelvic floor feels like it is burning now, stretched to the maximum. This is known as the "ring of fire."

PUSH

Her head comes out. The pain immediately stops. After fifteen and a half hours of pain, it amazes me, this absence of pain. I forgot how delicious it feels to not be in pain. How could I take this for granted? I begin to come out of my cocoon.

With what feels like my last bit of strength and bravery, I push again. Her body easily slides out. She's a purple, bedraggled, bent thing. Her ankles and wrists are flexed. Her head is squeezed nearly as long as her torso. She looks fragile, like something in a jar in science class. The room is silent. Ann deftly puts her onto her back and gives her two puffs of oxygen. The purple thing cries loudly. My heart beats again. *When did it stop? Where did she learn to cry?* Our uniformed audience cheers. I'd forgotten they were here. We all laugh except Madison, who cries louder. My cocoon falls away. Its job is done.

As the emergency workers leave, I hear myself say, "Thank you for coming." My husband teases me later about having "impeccable manners even while bloody and nude."

As planned, I nurse her right away to start my milk. *When did I take my clothes off?* It takes some coaching and bending and pulling. "Lean forward," Ann says, "and put your nipple into her mouth." My back aches from leaning over and trying to nurse while still sitting on the plastic sheet on the carpet in our den. Finally, we get it started, and Madison takes it from there. Compared to other nursing stories I've heard, ours is very successful. She's soon sucking away. *Where did she learn that?*

Now I see how lovely she is. Barry says, "Hello, Madison," and she turns without letting go of the nipple to look at him. She knows his voice. I try it. I am surprised how squeaky I sound. "My baby," I say. She looks at me. Wow. A minute ago, she looked like a fetus. Now she is a baby, a human, who can suck and hear and see and, oh my God, she is beautiful.

Her tiny hand wraps itself around my finger like she's about to hit a rock-solid forehand. Barry and I stay up until midnight with her lying in our bed between us. We are exhausted but too excited to sleep. We can't stop staring at the amazement that is her.

At midnight, Barry falls asleep. I finally feel ready to sleep too, but what if Madison needs us? What if something happens to her? I couldn't stand to live without her. The thought slashes at my heart. Then I remember that I'd thought, just for a split but achingly clear second, that it would be okay if she died. Tears of pain and shame come quickly. I didn't know then about the animal inside me. That a mama bear—even a reluctant mama bear—will always put herself in harm's way to protect her child. It is obvious to me now that I will happily spend the rest of my life protecting her from any danger.

Madison and I lie in bed listening to Mozart's "A Little Night Music." Her tiny pink mouth, beautifully formed with high peaks like her father's, tugs away at my breast. She and the violins coax the milk up from deep within me. And the air is thick and sweet and soft.

The Beginning of the World

Anika Fajardo

I was born on the day the world was created. I grew up as an only child, the sun around which my single mother and doting grandparents orbited. I was never entirely sure I wanted a baby because having children would surely mean giving up my place as the center of the universe. So when my labor began on a Saturday in late October, the urgency and intensity of the pain felt like treason. One part of me was betraying the desires of the other.

The discomfort seeped in before dawn and rose with the daylight. The throbbing came and went, and then it came. A rope tightened around my abdomen and lower back. My organs had been taken over by a complex system of pulleys and ratchets. The bedroom walls we had painted in summer closed in on me with their ugly beige-ness. I gagged at the smell of cereal on my husband's breath.

"I don't want to do this," I told Dave, shaking my head as a contraction gripped me. "You do it."

When we bought our little foursquare house on a shady block in Minneapolis, I chose the paint colors and picked out which of the three bedrooms would be ours. The other two rooms became our separate offices. Dave got the smallest room, a tiny closet-sized space. "This could be the nursery someday," a friend said when she saw his room filled with amps and stacks of guitar cases.

"I'm not sure if we're going to have kids," I said. I had been repeating this for several years. I was happy with Dave. I wasn't convinced that a family needed a baby.

By the time we arrived at the hospital, I was already exhausted from the relentless pounding in my lower back and abdomen. I waited in the quiet of the high-ceilinged lobby as Dave parked the car. There were no other patients on this gray Saturday; I was left to suffer through each contraction with only a janitor for company. And even he was just passing through, wheeling a cart of supplies through the lobby and down a hallway.

The antiseptic smell and flickering of fluorescent lights reminded me of the time, nearly a decade earlier, when my grandfather developed a blood infection and spiked a fever. He was in his mid-seventies and was in good health otherwise, still fit and active, so it had been a shock to see him pale and gaunt in a hospital bed.

"Honey," he called from the bed when I walked in his room. The pale blue of the gown emphasized his pallor, and the crisp whiteness of the sheets made him look small and vulnerable. The table next to his bed was stacked with *New Yorker* and *Natural History* magazines, the ones he carried around everywhere in a leather satchel. While I sat talking to him, my mother and grandmother left the room to find coffee in the hospital cafeteria.

"Did you know, honey," he said after they had left, "that the world was created on your birthday?" He reached for a magazine. "Some guy," he went on, "figured out the exact date of the beginning of the world. October twenty-third."

In the hospital where I gave birth, the maternity floor's registration clerk was cordoned off behind a half-wall. She sat behind a sliding glass window that she could close, presumably to shut out the cries of laboring women.

"Name?" she said. Her hands were poised above her keyboard, and I glared at her, wincing through another bout of pain. How could she expect me to answer? Dave stepped to the window and gave her my vital information as I leaned on the ledge of the counter and let the pulsing seize me.

We were shown to a small, dark room with a bed, like a throne, in the center.

"You can change into this," a nurse said, handing us a hospital gown.

Dave helped me out of my maternity sweatpants and onto the bed. I concentrated on my survival. Breathe in. Breathe out. Curse. I wasn't thinking about some bullshit miracle of bringing a baby into the world. I was thinking about me.

When the nurse came back, she said, "If you want an epidural for the pain, we need to do it now."

We had talked about not using meds. Dave and I had researched the options and weighed the pros and cons of epidurals and gases for pain relief. We had practiced visualizations and breathing. In the 1950s, my grandmother had been one of the early adopters of natural childbirth, and when my mother was pregnant with me in the 1970s, she had practiced Lamaze breathing and declined any artificial help during labor. Dave looked at me for a cue.

I nodded. "Now," I said.

I appreciated the speed with which the nurse left to carry out my demand.

Soon, another nurse walked us down a hallway to the labor room, which had a view of industrial buildings. The streets below were gloomy and vacant. I felt like the last person in the world, the queen bee, the one who had to perform the duty of populating the city again.

"You're going to sit on the edge of the bed," the anesthesiologist told me, "and lean forward while I insert the catheter in your back."

"He has to leave," I said above the contractions, pointing to Dave. "He faints."

Before we were married, Dave and I had gone to see *Pulp Fiction* in a crowded movie theater. We were in the middle of the back row, where we had an unobstructed view of the screen. In the film, Uma Thurman's character has a drug overdose and the prescribed remedy is a shot of adrenaline, administered straight to the heart. John Travolta's character holds a huge syringe over her, its five-inch needle dripping, and plunges it in. Next to me, Dave shuddered and then slumped forward, head to knees.

"Let's go," I whispered in the theater. "Do you have to throw up?" I shook his arm and he bolted upright.

"I'm fine," he whispered back. "I just fainted."

So in the labor room, I didn't want him there while the needle was being inserted into the epidural space in my spine. I didn't want any distractions from me; I wanted all the attention, all care focused on me.

When the anesthetic took effect and I was feeling only the force of the contractions, not their stabbing, I was hungry. I told the nurse, "I want a steak and a baked potato."

But she said I wasn't allowed to eat.

"A glass of wine?" I tried.

The nurse ignored me. She came and went, preparing equipment and instruments just out of my sight. Dave held my hand and then stood by the window to watch the gray day. Then the pain, which had been dulled for an hour or two, slowly and inexplicably returned, inch by inch. A nagging ache turned into a sharp throbbing that radiated from my lower back and down my legs. In sixth-grade science class, I had collected insects, killed them in jars of alcohol, and pinned them to a sheet of white and crumbly Styrofoam. The dead insects had been suspended on colorful ball-head pins, and now, as the twisting spasms tried to contort my body, I felt as if I had been captured, a round beetle tied down by tubes and monitors.

"Keep breathing," the nurse said.

"Do you want music?" Dave asked. He had made a CD of soothing songs in preparation for this moment. Adrian Legg, Leo Kottke, Yo-Yo Ma. He popped the disc into the boom box he had hauled in from the car. Quiet acoustic guitars and gentle moans of cello and strumming mandolins circled and spun. The pain seemed worse, amplified by having been absent for a time. I closed my eyes, listened to the music, breathed. I let the whole thing wash over me and then I opened my eyes, suddenly annoyed at Dave's ministrations and the constant mandates from the nurse.

"Turn that thing off," I told Dave.

I turned to the nurse. "Do you know," I said as rudely as I could, "that wallpaper border is the ugliest thing I have ever seen."

The border was blue and pink, its colors left over from the early nineties, insipid and faded. It felt like an insult to what I was trying to do here.

The nurse laughed. "When you fill out the evaluation about your care here, be sure to mention the wallpaper," she said.

I almost laughed too, but another twist of my contracting uterus caught my breath and snatched it from me. The pain was intense and alive. It controlled me. I thought about dying. Did the universe contort and convulse like this, I wondered, when it was created?

"Push," the doctor finally said after three hours of this writhing and wishing.

"Bear down," said the nurse.

I thought of my grandmother making bread, folding and kneading the dough with well-floured hands. My whole body felt like that dough, the pain clawing at me. I wasn't thinking about steaks anymore. I lifted my knees to my chest and thought about the movie scenes of actresses pretending to give birth. I imitated their faces, but I wasn't sure what I was actually supposed to do. I felt like a character in a story.

"How's your pain level?" the nurse asked, looking not at me but at the pump beside me. "On a scale of one to ten?"

"A twenty," I said.

She fiddled with the dials and buttons, the magical increments that were supposed to give me relief.

"How about now?"

I felt the same; the same snaking pain lashed at me. "A nineteen," I said because I didn't want to be uncooperative.

"Okay, we can see the head," the doctor said. "Black hair."

I had also come out with black hair. Black hair and dark eyes and an impossibly round face. Round like the sun. I was the sun, I thought.

Then the doctor said, "Looks like the baby is posterior."

"What does that mean?" Dave asked, letting go of my hand for a moment.

"Face up," said the doctor. "We need to do a caesarean."

"No!" I was adamant. "I can feel everything," I cried.

The doctor looked at me. It was nearly midnight on a Saturday, and I wondered where else she could have been at that moment. She sighed, and I realized that I wasn't unique. The new mother who didn't want surgery after twelve hours of labor. She'd seen all this before.

"Do you want this baby to come out?" she asked.

I leaned back against the pillows. I wasn't sure. I wasn't sure I wanted to be a mother, and if the baby didn't come out, I would never have to be one. My life would not have to move forward or change.

"Let's get her prepped," the doctor said to the nurses, and it was all out of my control.

I was transferred to a gurney, and Dave was led away to change into scrubs and eat peanut-butter sandwiches meant to fortify him. He was gone and I was being wheeled down a corridor, the white tubes of light on the ceiling passing in front of my vision like telephone poles down a highway.

Once in the operating room, the anesthesiologist who had just come on duty discovered that the catheter had slipped out of the epidural space. Without the anesthetic running through my spine, I had been experiencing unmedicated labor, as if I had been foolish enough to do the whole thing as naturally as my mother and grandmother had done.

"I can't have surgery without something," I said. I envisioned a knife, a large kitchen knife, cutting through the flesh of my distended belly.

"We're going to have to do a spinal block," she told me. "This isn't ideal, doing a block after an epidural."

I sat on the edge of the operating table, hugging the obstetrician, my swollen feet dangling over the white tile. The anesthesiologist poked and prodded at my lower back even as contractions gripped me. The needle was going into my spine, but it couldn't seem to locate the magical sub-arachnoid space. So I kept talking as if talking, storytelling, would give me strength.

"My husband has a big head," I told the doctor as I clung to her neck, breathing in her smell of shampoo and antibacterial foam. "We can never find hats to fit him."

The OB/GYN looked down at me. "Never marry someone with a big head."

At last the spinal block took hold and they laid me down on the table, a nurse at my head, her hands outstretched as if to catch me should I fall. I heard the doctors and nurses and knew there was a bed and warming lamp for whatever would be pulled from me. And then I felt myself going numb—no, that's not what it was; numbness suggests a sensation, and I was experiencing a complete absence of feeling. The anti-feeling started at my stomach and lower back and moved its way up. My fingers, my arms, my chest. It moved into my ears, my chin, my cheeks. It began to take hold of my breathing, my mouth.

"Help," I cried out. "I can't breathe."

It was a bad dream, the kind where you try to scream but no sound comes out, the kind where you try to run, but your feet won't move.

"Help," I said in a whisper, all feebleness. And then I wasn't thinking anymore, not about babies or mothers or galaxies.

"Keep breathing," the nurse said. "It's okay."

And then everything went out.

In his hospital room, my grandfather kept talking about the creation of the world. He had fumbled with the glossy pages of the magazine, his hands wrinkled and spotted brown as if chocolate ice cream had melted over his knuckles. A large white bandage covered the catheter hub that carried the antibiotics to his bloodstream.

"It says here that this bishop—James Ussher—spent the end of his life calculating the dates and times for human history. All based on the Bible. Imagine."

I nodded.

"The twenty-third of October. Your birthday," he said. "Well, of course he calculated a different year: 4004 BC. So you were born on the day the world was created, honey."

When my grandfather tired, I left his side and went out into the corridor.

"How was he?" my mother asked anxiously.

"Fine," I said. "He told me my birthday is the beginning of the world."

My mother and my grandmother exchanged worried looks. "He's sicker than I thought," my mother said.

But he had been telling me stories since I was six or seven, and I believed them all. Sometimes, when I would stay over- night at my grandparents' house, I would wake up and see the kitchen light was on. My grandfather would be sipping a huge mug of the warm milk he drank for his insomnia and reading back issues of the *New Yorker*. I would tiptoe into the kitchen, and he would make me a cup of milk and tell me the stories.

It was like trying to swim out of a black hole, that coming out of the netherworld. Like a surreal dream that only feels like reality. I was reluctant to open my eyes, as if it would be easier to just fall back and let myself plunge into nothingness.

"It's a girl," I heard from somewhere. But I didn't know what those words meant.

"It's a girl," Dave said.

I opened my eyes and was blinded by lights. Lights like the big bang of the universe, the explosion of atoms and particles that created the world as we eventually came to know it.

"Look," I heard him say. But I didn't see anything, just the shapes and shadows of the recovery room. I closed my eyes again.

I awoke again later when the nurse brought my baby to me, laid her in my arms. We were in a new room, and Dave was asleep in the fold-down chair beside my bed. With the glow of the hall light, I could see the baby's face, small and round. A cherub nose like all babies have, slits of eyes, thin lips. Her hands were little claws, impossibly small, like a fairy's. I looked up to see the clock on the wall tick to four in the morning.

"This is my new life," I said. Or maybe I just thought it.

The next day my throat was scratchy from the intubation. When the doctors and nurses came to take my blood pressure and monitor my urinary output, they didn't tell me I was lucky. They didn't tell me how controversial it is to administer a spinal block following an epidural. They didn't mention that patients can die from what I later learned was called accidental total spinal analgesia. They watched me carefully, though. They gave me opiates and tended my staples.

My mother was the first of the visitors; she looked so normal in her coat and gloves. For some reason, I had expected that everything and everyone would be different now. But my mother was still my mother. She leaned over the bassinet in the hospital room and scooped up the baby.

I watched my mother cradle my daughter's head, hold her at arm's length, each of them trying to focus on the other. Then the baby began to fuss, and Dave laid her back in the bassinet to change her diaper.

"Look at those toes," my mother said, watching. While Dave practiced his new skill of diaper changing, she took hold of one of the baby's feet, held it in her hand. The feet were wrinkled and pink. They were padded on the tops and bottoms, and my mother looked as if she wanted to put one in her mouth. "They are just like yours were. We used to call them little tamales."

Later that day my grandparents arrived at the hospital. They brought champagne.

"Nursing mothers shouldn't have any champagne," the brusque nurse taking my blood pressure said. "No amount of alcohol is safe."

"But it's her birthday!" my mother cried. She poured the sparkling wine into plastic hospital cups.

It was my thirty-second birthday. The beginning of the world. Even though I had been usurped, I still had one more day of being lauded and serenaded. "*Happy birthday to you*," sang my family, my grandmother's wobbly harmonization coming in for the finale.

The little creature lay in my arms as they sang, her fists clenched as if she were still hanging on for dear life. I was learning to nurse this tiny, scrawny being. My breasts were engorged and tight with milk, and the baby's mouth was so small. I latched her toothless gums around my nipple and felt less like the center of the universe and more like the center of *her* universe. I was only beginning to understand the significance of this moment, of this new life. It would take time. For now, I sipped the champagne, and the cold bubbles shocked and startled.

Quiet Enough

Danielle Leshaw

I sent my husband away for the home birth. "Take our son and go," I said.

I wasn't angry. In fact, I was as calm as I'd ever been. The timing, I thought, was exactly right. My husband's sister was getting married. The wedding was two states away. We packed some luggage, and he asked again if he and our son should stay home instead. "Don't you need us?" he asked, sorting a pile of laundry. "This seems wrong. I should be here."

"No," I said. "I don't need you." Maybe there are times when such a statement is cruel, but in our case, my independence, my need for solitude, was simply a truth my husband and I both acknowledged. Still, I wished he'd stop making me say it.

We organized starched shirts and clean socks, dress shoes our son wasn't accustomed to wearing. My husband shook his head. "I don't think I'm going to succeed in getting him into this outfit." He held up a little yellow and white argyle sweater from Talbots. I laughed and thought: *Good luck, dear husband. We've each got work to do this weekend.*

My son and I hadn't ever been away from one another. He was still nursing. I wondered what my breasts would do

while he was gone and another child emerged from my body.
I worried my nipples would go dry. I prayed I could provide
for this newborn. I could have done some reading or asked the
midwife, but I was done reading about my body and asking for
wisdom. I was focused on getting this baby out in the quietest
way possible, and that meant not speaking very much or asking any more questions.

My husband and son finally left. I was alone in our home
for the first time in two years. Their scents were all around,
but not their loud ways. One without the other. I missed them,
but I delighted in the isolation. After cleaning and napping
and getting the home birth stuff in order, I went to my office
on campus. I was of two minds. The first told me that, with
a nursing newborn, I would be back in my office very soon,
because I was absolutely intuitively convinced that I would
stand up after this birth and life would move along, uninter-
rupted, simply with a new babe to hold and love. The other
mind told me to get my office organized since the universe—
a chaotic place—doesn't always honor our intuition.

I filed and cleaned and scribbled handwritten notes to
my staff. Then I decided, somewhat last minute, to accept an
invitation from a faculty member in the School of Art to watch
a Jewish performance artist who was visiting for the weekend. I locked the building, drove to the other side of campus,
and entered the grand hallway of the university museum.
The performance artist, butch and loud, wore a tuxedo with a
bright red bowtie and asked us all to do the cha-cha and the
limbo and to find a partner for a slow dance. She found me.
She put her hands around my waist and in the entryway of the
Kennedy Museum, with its chandeliers and pink walls and

marble tile, she twirled me and dipped me and kissed me on the lips and whispered, *Oh, baby.*

A French obstetrician, Dr. Michel Odent, has in recent years discouraged men from entering the birthing room. "The best environment I know for an easy birth is when there is nobody around the woman in labor apart from a silent, low-profile, and experienced midwife," he told the BBC in 2009. "Oxytocin," he went on to say, "is the love drug which helps the woman give birth and bond with her baby. But it is also a shy hormone and it does not come out when she is surrounded by people and technology."

After dancing with the performance artist, I drove home in our Volkswagen Bus and noticed how empty the town seemed for eight o'clock on a Friday night. At each intersection, the walk signs blinked, but nobody was around to respond. The thing about Athens, Ohio, is that occasionally a festival of some sort emerges to celebrate things like the local pawpaw fruit or music legend Willie Nelson, and the entire town, it seems—collectively, as if in a trance—gets in their cars and drives to a remote location with lakes and campgrounds. If there ever were a time to loot Athens, it would be during one of these festivals. Criminals could walk down the street and enter homes and steal TVs and jewels and nobody would be around to notice.

It just so happened that on the night of my daughter's emergence into the world, my midwife was at such a festival. She had warned me this might be the case. Out of cell phone range. Grooving with the rest of the hippies. And there I was, bouncing and dilating on the big blue birthing ball and even periodically going into the backyard to look at the full moon. I wanted the midwife to take her time. Maybe she'd show up just as I hit ten centimeters. Maybe I'd be lucky enough to be almost alone. If I couldn't be alone, I thought, a few women who knew how to be quiet would suffice.

My mother, who in the days of my youth was an outspoken feminist, had driven me to my first gynecological appointment before I even had my period. From her spot in the driver's seat, she told me that this was women's work. "Don't ever go to a male gynecologist, understand?" She looked at me instead of looking at the road. I listened and swore on my life, and I knew that with that swearing, she expected me also to pass this important information on to whatever daughters I might be lucky enough to birth sometime in the imaginary future.

During high school, my Irish Catholic friend was taken by *her* mother to *her* first gynecological exam not because a relationship with a doctor was essential for a menstruating teenager, but because her mother suspected sexual activity. When she told me that her doctor was a man, I was confused, then outraged. How dare a man poke and prod my best friend! How dare a male doctor feel her breasts for lumps! I had begun to reason, even as a teenager, that these areas should only be touched either by women doing important medical work or by people designated as your romantic partner. Twenty-five years later, I still feel the same way.

Which brings me to the first of two big lies. In order to ensure that I would only be seen by a female doctor, I lied to the OB/GYN practice and said I was too religious to have any man touch my body other than my husband. As the only rabbi in all of Athens, and usually the only rabbi they've ever met face-to-face, I can get people to believe anything I say. Thus

I always got, for every prenatal exam, the one female doctor, who is the most beloved doctor in all of Athens. I did this not because I was "too religious" but because I couldn't imagine the sixty-five-year-old male doctor, with his cowboy boots and handlebar mustache, peering into my vagina. And here's the other lie: I told the doctor I planned to have a hospital birth. If the beloved female doctor had known I was planning a home birth, she would've dismissed me from her practice. I lied in order to see the doctor, and then I lied in order to keep her.

Ohio state law isn't friendly to midwives, especially lay midwives, and large OB/GYN practices aren't friendly to the idea that a client might be interested in utilizing a lay midwife. I was informed that I would be dismissed from the practice if I were planning a home birth. I wanted prenatal care, including ultrasounds, but I also wanted a doctor who knew me— "backup" in case my home birth didn't go as smoothly and safely as planned.

This adored female doctor and I made small talk, and I didn't mention the midwife or her assistant or how they were also doing a series of prenatal exams and handing me lists of things to do, like put several baby blankets in the oven and bake them in brown paper bags at 350 degrees. Our first child had emerged easily. Some intense contractions at home, a late-night drive to the hospital, a bit of pushing on the birthing stool, and out he slid into his dad's hands. Four hours from start to finish. Because of this first birth, I felt certain the second baby could be born at home. I'd get to avoid all the loud moments, like the beeping machines and the nurses asking me to rate my pain on a scale from one to ten. I wanted a quiet and private birth, preferably in the bathtub with the lights dim.

Several hours after my husband and son left for the week-end, I asked the OB/GYN to scrape my membranes.

"Are you sure?" she asked. "We're still two weeks away."

"I'm enormous. The baby is ready. Let's get this show on the road."

She didn't need much convincing. In went her fingers. Around and around and around. All I could do was pray that it would work and that I would have this baby while my husband and son were far away at the family wedding. I knew my window of solitude was small. They would be gone for just seventy-two hours.

The doctor was hopeful. "That should get things going," she said. "I'm on call for the next few nights. So the next time I see you, we'll be having a baby." She smiled. She had freckles. Oh, how I liked her! Which is why I left that afternoon feeling my most horrible. I felt certain that this baby was going to come out smoothly and gently. I imagined that in the life of an OB/GYN, the easy births, without any snipping or screaming or chaos, were the moments of experiential relief and gratitude. I was doing my best to rob her of that gift.

Later that evening, roughly eight hours after visiting the doctor, I bounced on my birthing ball and scribbled down contractions and wondered when the midwife would decide she'd had enough music and fresh air. She finally got my voice-mail and called me back to ask how things were progressing. She told me she was still at least thirty minutes away, deep in the woods of Appalachia. No problem, I replied, and in that moment it was true.

The week before, I had bumped into a woman in the super-market who told me, while we were standing next to the late-summer watermelons, that she had simply filled the bath and pushed her baby out all by herself while the midwife was in transit.

"Totally alone?" I asked in disbelief.

"Yes," she said, "and it was the most beautiful alone I've ever experienced." I left the watermelons and imagined my own solo birthing expedition. Me in my bathtub, the water muffling my heavy breathing. I'd push, then pull a baby up and out. I'd nurse her until somebody arrived to help us out of the water. It seemed perfect!

I could have guaranteed such an arrangement. No one made me call the midwife. I suppose it was fear that caused me to reach out. I had to let someone know what was going on, and I owed it to my husband to have assistance with the birth, but still I prayed, in the moments after I hung up with the midwife, that she wouldn't make it to the house in time. That *I* would get to experience the most beautiful alone.

But a part of me was scared, and in the end, some things aren't meant to be. Thirty minutes later, the team arrived. I welcomed the midwife and her assistant and then my dear friend and even her husband, who dropped by to deliver a new package of batteries for the portable heart monitor and left just as quickly. The three women filled the tub and dimmed the lights, and I stepped into the water while they sat on the floor. It turned out all three women had been at the festival. I laughed. That festival had almost granted me the solitary birth I wasn't sure I wanted until I stood near the watermelons in the grocery store. But these women were giving me the next best thing.

Without my having to ask, they knew to be really, really quiet. My ears were partially submerged, just enough that I heard the *whomp whomp* of my body turning from side to side, easing the pain. I took a nap but woke up, begging for the labor to end. Finally, when I thought I couldn't take any more pain, a baby swam out and up and the midwife placed her on my breast. I opened my eyes and looked at her quiet little face. When I peeked between her legs, I think I sighed with relief.

There are things we know. We don't know how we know them. This birth had been that way since the beginning. I knew it would be gentle. I knew it would be at home. I knew whatever baby emerged from my womb would emerge easily and without cries or tears. The piece that was never entirely clear in my vision was who would be present. There were days I had hoped my little boy would see his baby sibling born. There were times I thought I could coach my husband into being in the space so beautifully that I would appreciate his presence and whatever words he had to say. But the thing about my husband is that he chats when he's nervous. And chatting, though I had endured it during the first birth, wasn't an option for the second birth.

My husband jokes that I need a sensory deprivation chamber, that I should walk the earth with plugs in my ears. There's some truth to this. I find the world a noisy place. I rarely, if ever, listen to music. Crowds aren't about people; they're about the sound level. In general, I find unnecessary conversation an assault on my eardrums. I often fantasize about weeklong silent meditation retreats. *Please, can everybody just stop talking?*

I stepped out of the bath water to put on my pajamas and climb into bed. The midwife asked if I wanted anything to eat. "Yogurt? Cheese?" She and her assistant and my friend were all standing at the foot of the bed.

"No," I said. "Really. I'm great."

It was three in the morning. They'd been in the house for almost four hours. My husband and son would arrive home the following evening. All I wanted was to be alone. "Thank you," I said. "I've got everything I need." There was, after all, a sweet little baby face peeking out of a swaddled blanket, and the rest of the family was on their way home. I asked the midwife and her attendants to leave, so they gathered their things and shut off the lights and locked the door behind them. I wondered if I had been rude to kick them out so quickly. Years later, I would also wonder if I actually could have gone through with it. Could I have been like the woman I met beside the watermelons? Could I have given birth all by myself? But what I never question is that with the return of the men, exhausted from their own journey to wedding fanfare and back, there was enough quiet for then, enough time alone for me and my new daughter.

Skin Time

Becki Melchione

After eight and a half months, our long-distance, nontraditional pregnancy is ending today. Our gestational carrier, Heather, has just been wheeled into the surgical delivery room. She has been calm, lying on the hospital bed in the center of the pre-op room, watching the clock and wondering when they would finally bring her in for the C-section. It was scheduled for noon. We have been here since eleven.

Her husband Jon, my husband Luc, and I are left in the pre-op room waiting. Jon, a large bald truck driver with not an insignificant number of tattoos, had been holding her hand, caressing it softly. He is a professional at being there for her for this, her fourth time giving birth. Of course, this time is different: it's a surgical delivery, it's twins, and they're not hers. Now he waits with us as the hospital staff prepares Heather for her C-section. We try to make nervous small talk, but there's not much to say. We're just waiting—us to have our children and him to have his wife back. Eventually a nurse appears and says, "Jon, come with me."

He grins at Luc. "It's time," he says. "Are you ready?"

Left alone, Luc and I pace, glancing at each other and the walls that seem to be getting closer and closer. Minutes stretch

into an infinity of silence and nervous glances. Long waits in a
hospital portend the worst, I think. I learned that the hard way,
waiting patiently, obliviously, while the doctors reviewed my
records and tests before determining the worst. "Cancer," they
whispered.

"Please, God," I repeat now, my prayers for my own health
forever replaced by prayers for my children's.

Finally, a nurse comes to escort us into the room where our
miracle will happen. We follow like eager puppies, so excited
we're nearly peeing on the floor.

My husband and I are guests here, let in at the last possible minute. A demand from our very pregnant Heather
had worked: "But they're the *parents*! They have to be in the
room!" This was the one part of our birth plan that had to
be left undetermined. Although Heather was adamant that
we be in the delivery room, no one in her obstetrician's office
was sure which anesthesiologist would be on call that day,
and we were told it was his or her decision who could be in
the room. In the waiting room, we had tried to look sympa-
thetic, but we looked more anxious than anything. We had
driven eight and a half hours from Baltimore the day before,
gobbled down our last dinner as parents-to-be, and stayed at
the hotel across the street from the hospital. Neither of us had
slept, so we unpacked, reviewed, and repacked the bags of
new baby clothes and blankets that we had brought to bring
to the hospital.

Part of the reason we chose this hospital was that the doctors
and staff have a good record of working with surrogates and

their intended parents. They are, in third-party reproduction parlance, "surrogacy friendly." They will place our names on the birth certificates so we won't have to adopt our daughters months after their birth. We'll be treated as the parents, with doctors and nurses giving *us* the updates and reports and asking *us* to make the medical decisions when needed. The hospital has arranged two rooms next door to each other—one for Luc, me, and our babies, and one for Heather, so we can all share the first few days together.

Doctors and nurses crowd the surgical suite. I begin to count—*one, two, three, four, five, six*—but they are all sheathed in green and blue scrubs, identical except for their faces. They move swiftly, checking machines, equipment, all of the patients. I lose my place. I want to remember every detail of this moment so I can write about it later. Really, though, the number of doctors and nurses doesn't matter. They're the supporting characters. I'm desperate to see the stars of this show.

I stand with my back to the wall, trying not to be in the way. I have my camera. I'm ready to document. Part of me still can't believe that we've reached this moment, that our triumph against all of the obstacles we had no idea how to surmount has finally come. I'm about to see the birth of my daughters.

Then there are waves of fear—not just that there could be a complication during the birth or that my life will be forever different as a parent, but that something horrific could happen. My paternal grandfather died on the day he was to be released from the hospital. My maternal grandfather went into the emergency room for something he thought was minor and never left. When I went to the hospital for emergency surgery for a detached retina, I learned that I had been misdiagnosed and that what had been missed was far, far worse than what I was supposed to have fixed. The feeling that bad things happen in hospitals has never left me.

Maternity wards are the good part of the hospital, I repeat to myself over long breaths in and out. *Everything will be okay.*

Luc, a physician, is comfortable in this element. With our video camera, he strides closer to the unfolding scene, an array of people and machines. I'm the photographer. He's the videographer.

This wasn't the way we envisioned having our first child. We tried the usual route, starting the month after we returned from our honeymoon. First I miscarried. Then doctors diagnosed me with a rare cancer of the eye that was even rarer for a thirty-four-year-old. Between the cancer and the treatment to cure it, my vision in that eye was destroyed. Color drained from the world; blues and greens submerged into a murky gray while bright reds, yellows, and oranges, the colors of summer roses and autumn leaves, toned down to burnt umber. I could not see anything if there was too much light or darkness. Riding in a car at night, I was pummeled by streetlights, strobes disrupting my brain's ability to make out shapes. It was like being torpedoed into space, surrounded by blackness and the starlight only illuminating itself.

That eye cancer would compromise my ability to procreate never crossed my mind. At first, I was focused on surviving. One of the seven stages of grieving is bargaining, and I bargained like a market vendor. I offered up my vision, and the universe guaranteed I'd have another thirty years. When I felt relatively confident that cancer hadn't shortened my life, that there was the possibility I would have the family I so desperately wanted, I worried about who would drive my future children around at night because I knew, now that I was half-blind, that I wouldn't. It had taken me months to drive in the daylight again and over a year to drive at night, and though I was cautious, new scratches and dings appeared regularly on my car, the result of my spatial misjudgments and miscalculations. For me, driving at night was not just uncomfortable but risky, and though I didn't anticipate having to do it often, I imagined scenarios with Luc working late or being on a trip while each daughter had a different activity on the other side of town.

Bathed in light on the operating table, Heather's calm face belies any anxiety she may feel. Jon stands by her head, behind the curtain that separates her head and chest from the rest of her body. "So what's going on down there?" she wonders aloud as we enter the room. I'm overwhelmed by the reality of the gifts we are about to receive, and when I look at Heather, she says, "Oh, you're going to make me cry, too!"

Numb from the chest down, she glows with excitement. This, she had told me weeks before, is her favorite part. She relishes the spotlight, the activity all focused on her. "I should have had my girls via C-section. Nobody told me it was this easy. I don't even have to do anything. Becki, from now on, you're going to have the hard part!"

As she chatters, the doctors make the incision, clamping open the skin and layers of flesh. "Here's Baby A," the doctor announces, holding it up like a trophy before handing off the wriggling creature. A nurse clamps the umbilical cord and snips her free. Another nurse wraps her in blankets, wipes off the white vernix and reveals a speckled pink and blue and white baby girl. Whisked to a warming table, Baby A shouts, angry at the piercing air, bright lights, and unfamiliar textures. The nurse announces her an eight.

An eight? I think. *What does that mean? She's perfect. Shouldn't she be a ten?*

The nurse reassures me. "I'll check again in a few minutes. An eight is good."

Then I remember it, from *What To Expect When You're Expecting.* The Apgar, of course. Timidly, I ask the nurse, "Can I touch her?"

"Yes," she says. "She's yours!"

Mine. I hold out a single finger and tentatively reach toward the warm skin of her arm, her wrist, her hand. She feels like warm, buttery silk. I worry that I'll snag her skin as I slide my fingertip toward her palm. I can't help but want to touch her. She's looking for some comfort, too. Her fingers embrace my fingertip. It's just a reflex, but I'm still in awe. I hold my hand above her face to shield her eyes from the bright light, and she opens them just enough to see my face smiling at her. I'm a stranger. My voice isn't the one she's heard for the last nine months in utero, so I introduce myself. "Hello, I'm Mom," I whisper, barely able to get the words out. "I've been waiting for you."

Two minutes disappear in the phenomenon that is Baby A. She weighs just over six pounds, with a head of peach fuzz and eyes the color of a stormy sky at dusk. She looks remarkably like the Cabbage Patch Kid Preemie I had when I was ten, round face and button nose. She makes it easy to forget that a second baby is on her way. My husband, so happy capturing Baby A's every reaction to her new world, turns to film our Baby B's arrival. I don't know where to look, so my head turns back and forth, back and forth, at the baby at my fingertips and the baby just arriving. It is my first glimpse of what being a mother to twins will be—two constantly vying for my attention, my deepest need to be everything for both.

"And here's Baby B," the doctor says. The video camera swings from one baby's first moments to the second baby's birth. "I feel so much lighter already!" Heather laughs, eliciting chuckles from Jon and the nurses attending her. Instantly, Luc is at Baby B's side.

"Look at her! She's beautiful!" he effervesces over Baby B's tiny feet. It's trite, but only because everyone does it. He starts quietly: "One, two, three . . ." Then he bellows, "There's ten toes!" According to the nurse, Baby B is a nine. She weighs two ounces less than her sister. Her face is a bit longer, her nose narrower and pert. They are fraternal twins, the result of two embryos. We study them both to search for the differences.

"They're both perfect," I say, mostly to myself. I'm in disbelief that I could be so lucky. Despite everything that threatened the possibility of this moment, still the time has arrived, and I am the most grateful, elated person on the planet. Then I remember the person who made this possible. Heather. She's watching us from across the room, smiling.

"How can I ever thank you?" I ask. Before we entered the delivery room, we gave her a pendant necklace with an expression of our gratitude engraved in pure silver. But it hardly feels like enough. Nothing could possibly be enough. "Just watching you is enough for me," she replies.

Baby B, now swaddled tightly, lolls in the cradle of my arms. Luc holds Baby A close, so only her sleeping face is visible in the soft blanket wrapped around her. He whispers a lullaby in his

native Spanish. Gold heart-shaped stickers marked A and B are
stuck to the pink-and-blue knit caps on the tops of their heads
so everyone—doctors, nurses, and parents—can easily tell them
apart. A nurse comes to take them. Neither of us is ready to let
them go. There's so much to catch up on already. We want to
study their faces, listen to their breath, hold their fingers.

"You'll get them right back," the nurse assures us as she lifts
the babies from our arms to place them side by side in rolling
cribs. Layered with pink-and-blue blankets, these will be their
beds for the duration of our hospital stay. She directs us out of
the bright lights and beeping machines of the surgical suite to
the cozy peace of the recovery room next door. "Skin time is a
great way to bond," she tells us.

In the recovery room, we are left alone with our daughters.
Stripped naked from the waist up, Luc and I sit in reclin-
ing chairs facing each other. Soft blankets wrap around our
shoulders and the newborns on our chests. Baby A grows quiet
as she absorbs Luc's warmth. Her eyelids flutter over irises that
will fade to match his aquamarine eyes. Baby B lies between
my breasts, directly above my heart; her body melts into mine.
Luc and I glance at each other, the bliss on both our faces
unmistakable. Then I close my eyes so it is just me and Baby B,
so I can absorb the feel of her skin on mine, how the soft rise
and fall of her body synchronizes with my breath. A thought
rises—that every pain, every disappointment, every unusual
thing we did leading to this moment was essential—and then it
disappears as she turns her head.

Boothville

Lisa Southgate

It started as an urge to clean my bedroom. Actually, it started with middle-of-the-night sex nine and a half months ago, but this particular morning began with me cleaning my bedroom, which has gotta be the first time I've ever done it without Mum yelling at me first. Next comes a bruised feeling that begins during *Ladyhawke*. Actually, lots of bruised feelings, all over. I try to ignore them and concentrate on the movie because Alan and Karen have brought it over especially for me, and they waited while I vacuumed and dusted and found one more thing to wipe down. "Come on, Lisa," Karen said. "We rented these for you, you know." And I said, "Yeah, yeah, nearly there." But I could not unwrap my hand from the Spray & Wipe bottle. Finally, Alan herded me into the lounge room and put me into the big brown beanbag, Karen put the videotape in the player, and they sank down to the couch and into their perpetual hug and said, "Now, you've got to watch carefully."

There's a gold sun, a blue moon, a brown hawk, and a screen full of something dark and indistinct, like a wall of mud. Then a clump of dirt falls away and a boy's head emerges, and he says, "It's not unlike escaping mother's womb. God, what a memory."

Alan and Karen laugh and laugh.

I don't. I'm finding it hard to follow things. I try to pay attention to the Alan Parsons Project soundtrack and the man with the double crossbow, but something keeps prodding me—a broom handle, it feels like. I shift and I'm okay for half a minute, and then there's another prod. The second movie is *Octopussy*, and I can't follow it at all. So Alan and Karen give up on me.

"Ha ha, you're in labor," Karen says as they leave.

I'm not sure. All day I'm not sure. But in the evening, another friend calls, and I tell her how I've been feeling. She hands the phone to her mum, a physiotherapist, who listens to my description—twinges, not in front but around the back, behind my hips—and says, "I think you're in labor." This is when I tell Mum.

"I like how you asked some stranger instead of me," Mum says.

It feels unfair. I didn't mean to ask someone else. It just happened, like so many things do.

Mum tells me to have a shower and make sure my hospital bag is in order, while she finishes getting dinner on for Dad and Granddad and my little brother, Steven.

Of course my hospital bag is in order. I packed it two months ago with things like the violet soap and violet talc my aunty brought me from Tasmania three years ago. I packed pretty, comforting things that would cheer me up. So I collect my bag, Mum and I get into the Bluebird, and eleven minutes later we are at Boothville.

Boothville, owned by the Salvation Army, is both a hospital and kind of a hostel for unmarried mothers. It's a big white mansion on the crest of one of the hills that surround inner-city Brisbane. The building is beautiful—bay windows, a rose garden, and an interior that smells of furniture polish and baby soap. I worked extra hours on the checkouts at Target to afford to come here because my doctor told me that at Boothville, they let you see the baby before they give it away.

The duty nurse weighs me and says, "You'll have a little baby." As if sixty-one kilos, 134 pounds, is petite. The pains are thirty minutes apart. Perhaps I'm too early. But no way am I going back home. So they settle me into a big, sparse delivery room with a narrow bed for me, a chair for Mum, and a cork floor that gleams expectantly. "We'll just wait and see what happens overnight," the duty nurse says.

I pull out my knitting.

I'd never knitted until three days ago, when I just felt like trying it. I've knitted a band of rose pink and a band of pea green. I'm not sticking to a pattern or anything. I'm just doing "knit one, purl one" over and over again. It's satisfying. I think I could be good at this.

"What are you knitting?" the nurse asks, coming in with a cup of tea for me.

"A blanket for my cat, Pepe."

The nurse glances at Mum.

"It's a very spoiled cat," Mum says.

I think of how, a month ago, Mum said, "Seeing how attached you are to Pepe, I don't think you're going to give this baby up."

"Yes, I will," I said. "It's not the same. I've had Pepe for years. I love him. The baby's a human that I've never met before."

My friends agree with Mum. Alan and Karen keep saying, "You won't be able to give it up. It's the hormones."

The hormones, the hormones. Like I'm nothing but a bunch of hormones, no brain, no will of my own. Like I'm weak. Like I'm one of those soppy women on TV who just fold into sobs when they see their babies for the first time. Like I'm a dumb woman who stays home all day and wears a floral cotton shift and watches *Days of Our Lives* and only goes outside to hang out her washing. Like I don't have anything else. Like I'm not going to be a *journalist*.

I've had that planned ever since grade ten, when one of my teachers said, "You like to write? You should be a journalist."

So I'm going to be a journalist. We're all going to have careers, all of us, all my friends. You don't question it. You just pick one. We're not living in the seventies anymore. On career day, there's no booth for motherhood. If you get pregnant, your next thought is not motherhood. It's *get rid of it*.

Abortion is still illegal in Queensland in 1985, but you can drive over the New South Wales border to Tweed Heads, where they use a little vacuum-cleaner thingy with a duck's bill. One of my friend's flatmates got on the phone and described the process to me—and offered me her little gold frequent customer card.

I did think about it. In those queasy, dreamlike days after the doctor's receptionist told me in a kind, worried voice, like I had cancer: "It's positive, love." There were home pregnancy tests, but I wouldn't have bought one. That in itself would have been too positive for me: yes. You are having sex. So I put up with being tired and washed out, and I imagined I had leukemia or AIDS or all sorts of things until the day of three asparagus-and-cheeses.

Walking from Central Station to my university campus—provided I didn't detour to my friend Peter's place and play Dungeons & Dragons—there's a network of arcades and cafes, and this day I stopped at one café after another and ordered asparagus and cheese on toast. I had to. After each one, I felt like I hadn't eaten anything at all. I couldn't think of anything but lovely melted cheese and pale, mushy, fresh-from-a-tin asparagus. At the last café, hidden in a little arcade at the top of Queen Street, I had it in a crepe.

And still, when I rang the doctor and got the results, I was shocked.

This didn't happen to me. *Life* didn't happen to me, not like it happened to other people. Life like this happened to people on TV, in a miniseries like *Lace*. But also, of course it bloody well happened to me, too. I should have seen this coming. I should have seen it coming months ago, when my half-elven druid fell pregnant to Peter's fighter/magic-user/thief.

I told my friends about my positive test. I couldn't help it. Alan, Karen, the other gamers, my old friends from high school, Peter, even some beanie-wearing guy at the Campus Club bar whom I'd only met once before. The beanie guy bought me a rum and Coke and gave me a lecture that finished in a crescendo of: "What right do you have to be a mother?" Then he made a pass at me.

Peter delivered a monologue about survival of the fittest. Implication: What's to say the mother can't be the hostile environment? This was his detached way of saying, *get rid of it*. Everyone was saying *get rid of it* even when they weren't saying it.

Except for one friend, who said, "You couldn't marry Peter, could you?"

Did those words really come from Mary-Anne? Mary-Anne, my best friend from school, who sometimes stood next to me and sang Olivia Newton-John songs into Impulse fragrance tins? She was suggesting I marry someone I didn't love? And who didn't love me?

I tried to picture marriage to Peter. Remote, handsome, selfish, chess-playing, perpetual-student Peter.

"He wouldn't do it," I told Mary-Anne. "It would be a disaster. *I* wouldn't do it."

"I mean," she said, "just to give the baby a name."

I realized the words weren't actually coming from her. They were coming from her mother and grandmother. They were words squeezed out of the sixties and the seventies. It was the shame of the 1950s right up against the ambition of the 1980s, and here I was standing on the crack.

Get rid of it. It sounds like it should be one word. *Get-rid-of-it.* It sounds like something you say when you're smoking in the bedroom and your mother's coming down the hallway. It sounds like stubbing out a cigarette and stuffing it down the bathroom sink.

I went around with *get-rid-of-it* in my head for two days. Sure, I could *get-rid-of-it*. I was just the same as everyone else. Wasn't I?

No, I wasn't.

I came to this realization lying in bed in my sister's old room. My sister had moved out two years before, and I took over her room even though I didn't like its pink walls. My room, with its green walls and horse pictures and clippings of John Travolta, had become too messy to sleep in. Here I had to look at a pink wall and a print with a big-eyed girl clutching a white kitten. Yet I spent a lot of time lying on this bed and listening to the frantic scrabble of my thoughts.

It hit me—somewhere in the middle of planning an "immaculate conception" defense—that the most terrifying part of being pregnant was not getting fat, and it wasn't the pain. It was confessing to Mum that I'd been having sex.

It was a huge thought. It made everything still—my mad mental panic, even my heart. Everything subsided except for a few lucid questions. What if that scary thing was not an issue? What if I took the sex confession out of my thinking for a second? What would I do?

I would have the baby. And I would adopt it out.

I felt a kind of release, the kind you feel after exertion. I'd moved something. Some dirt had fallen away. I could go straight through.

When I told Mum, she said, "You had your whole life ahead of you, and now you've stuffed it up."

Her voice sounded like brittle glass, breaking.

I was the first kid in our branch of the family to go to university.

"No, I haven't," I said quickly. I outlined the plan: I would keep studying until the end of this semester and take the next semester off. I would go to this place called Boothville. After I gave the baby up, I would go back to university and take on more subjects. I could *accelerate* along my career path. I could still be a journalist . . .

I talked until she stopped crying.

This morning, the pain is coming from behind, like a knife into my bottom vertebrae.

When a contraction comes, I drop my knitting and hold on to the sides of the bed and just try to turn myself into nothing, into air, until it passes. When it goes and I can breathe again, Mum has my knitting in her hands. "You've dropped a stitch. That will make a hole," she says, and fixes it. She hands it back and I continue until the next contraction. "Want me to pick up that stitch?" Mum says, and I nod painfully. But the contractions are coming so fast now. I can't have Mum continually fixing my mistakes. So I stop handing it over. I just keep knitting. Let the holes be holes. My contractions will always be visible as a line of holes in my knitting.

Someone brings me a cup of tea and two little yellow sugar sachets. The sachets are printed with quotes from famous thinkers. Mum picks one and reads: "One of the greatest pains to human nature is the pain of a new idea." She says, with that weird splat of humor that sometimes comes from her like a raindrop from a cloudless sky: "See, Lisa? It could be worse. You could be having a new idea."

I think it's a lame joke.

As a pain spasm ebbs away I hear Mum say, "Hello." I twist around and see Mary-Anne setting her little white plastic basket bag down on the cork floor. She's here to help, and she's all white and quiet about it.

I had no idea she'd come. I hadn't even thought of it. Mary-Anne can't stand hospitals, sickness, or spew—she can't even stand *to* spew. She holds it in. She clamps down on it. Except for that night we all got stuck into vodkas and Fanta at her flat. None of us could hold it in, and Mary-Anne certainly couldn't. She bolted for the veranda and spewed a fountain of orange vomit right onto someone's beautiful silver Datsun 280ZX.

Mum doesn't know Mary-Anne can't stand spew. She hands her my banana-shaped spew pan. Without a word, Mary-Anne takes it to the bathroom and washes it out.

I can't understand why this is so hard. I've prepared for it. Mum and I went to antenatal classes in Boothville's front parlor. There were about five couples there besides us, and we watched videos and listened to a talk and asked questions. We were told we could give birth any way we wanted. We could stand, squat, we could even deliver on a beanbag if we wanted to. We practiced the breathing, lying flat on the vintage rose carpet. We started with phase one, the long relaxed breaths. Slowly . . . breathe . . .

And then there was this long, choking sound from the carpet next to me. My mother was snoring. My mother was *asleep*.

I sat bolt upright, as if I were covered in ants. I couldn't look at anyone. I couldn't even look at Mum. How could she humiliate me like this?

I prodded her with my index finger. "Mum," I hissed. "Mum!"

"What? Oh. I wasn't asleep."

"Yes, you were!"

I heard a soft laugh. I looked around at the couple called Jamie and Barbara. Barbara was still smiling. She looked at me with eyes as clear and green as sunlight on a citrus leaf. She smiled right into me as if there was nothing weird about this. As if I were a grown-up, too.

I took home the handouts on breathing and I practiced. It's all done wrong on TV—those stupid women always start with quick, short puffs. That's the third stage. I will do it right.

Except I can't. There is nowhere for the breathing to occur. My body is squished between two planks of pain. It can't go forward, in a big breath, and it can't go back, in a cringe. I don't know where to put my body. Nothing works.

A midwife suggests we page my doctor.

I chose my doctor carefully. I made a shortlist of obstetricians, called each one, and crossed them off the list if I didn't like their manner, or their receptionist, or the sound of their name. I was left with a guy with footballer shoulders and a humorous brusqueness that made me feel safe. But now I am furious at him. What is he doing at some other hospital with some other patient? *Now*?

"He's only five minutes up the road, at the Royal Brisbane," the midwife tells me.

But that's too long. Pain is stretching out each minute like it's mozzarella.

When my doctor finally arrives, he tells me he will put me on a hormone drip to stimulate contractions and give me an epidural so that I don't feel them.

"Do you understand?" he asks me. "Is there anything else you want to know? Is there anything you want to ask me?"

He looks at me, and I notice that his eyes are the light gray of old aluminum. They are asking me to ask him something. Something specific.

"Will I need a caesarian?" I ask. I'm helping him out. He doesn't want to be the first to say the C-word. I don't know why—at this point I'd love one.

"We'll have everything standing by in case," he says. "But at this stage, no. The baby is not in distress."

"Well, I am!" I say, but he's already gone, off to another patient. I can't believe he won't just stay here with me. I don't understand why he can't just give me the epidural himself. But no, an anesthetist must administer it. That's another call to another pager, another wait for a phone call, and another wait for someone to travel here.

I come out of another set of contractions to discover a lunch tray next to my bed. It contains boiled peas, carrots, and a lamb chop. For the last nine months I've craved lamb chops. Now, nothing is more offensive. The round, rich smell of lamb fat grows and fills my whole world. I beg Mum to push the tray into a far corner. I will never eat lamb chops again.

Sometime in the afternoon, a cool, dry voice asks: "Does someone here want an epidural?" The anesthetist is a thin, unhurried man. He explains the risks to me, then retires to the corner of the room and washes his hands. Slowly. Minutely. I pant with each exhalation: "Hurry, hurry, hurry."

"That's not going to make me go any faster," he says.

After another eternity, he approaches. Then he folds me over onto my side. Mary-Anne runs out of the room.

In a few moments, the epidural bleeds through my body and lifts it out of all pain. I talk and entertain Mum with lines from "The Miracle of Birth," the first part of Monty Python's *The Meaning of Life*, and I feel I can take anything. I am myself again. But time, which stretched before, now shrinks. The pain returns. Sounds hurt. In the delivery room next to this, a family is getting ready for a birth. Children are squealing, running, sliding along the floor, thudding against the wall. It all hurts. I say something to Mum, who says something to a nurse. Next I hear a man yell, in angry tones, "There's a lady having a baby in the next room, so get back into your sleeping bags and pipe down, the lot of you!"

I am given another epidural. And, all too soon, another one. A phone rings in a room far away. A woman comes in and whispers to Mum the name of one of my Dungeons & Dragons friends. Does she want to take the call? No, Mum says.

My doctor's back. He's wearing a cap and mask and hooks my ankles into stirrups. Hey, what about the squatting, the beanbag, the choice?

"Sorry," he says. "We're way past that stage now."

I quote Monty Python at the doctor: the delivering mother in *The Meaning of Life*. "What do I do?"

And my doctor quotes back, "Nothing. You're not qualified."

The phone rings again, and a nurse detaches herself and goes away and comes back. She whispers another name to Mum. Another of my D&D friends. God, is the entire Gamers Guild calling, one by one?

My doctor concentrates. He has forceps, his movements are committed; he puts his torso into the job, he twists his foot-baller shoulders. I hear a sound like a quack from a grouchy little duck, and the doctor says, "It's a big boy." This baby is put in my arms.

The unexpected weight of him. His realness, his completeness, his well-drawn limbs, his mashed brown hair and sleepy
blue eyes. He looks around the room and back at me with a
heavy, skeptical gaze.

My face ripples, as if strummed . . . No. I will not cry like
those stupid women on TV. I clamp down on it. I know I'm being
watched. I touch the baby's tiny mauve toes, wrinkled as if he has
been in the bath. Is it all right that his toes are mauve and that his
fingers are burgundy? And the dark splash on his forehead?

It's all natural, I'm told. He's fine, they say. That's a birth-
mark, and it will fade. They call it the stork's footprint.

I think this is a very well-made baby.

I need to throw up. Someone takes him and, just in time,
slips a pan in front of me. I throw up and up. Someone asks
Mum if she would like to bathe the baby. I keep throwing up.
I'm on to my third spew pan now.

"Oh no. Look what you've done to your poor little
mummy," a nurse says.

"He doesn't care," Mum says, her voice all thin and
sing-song through the gentle splash of water. "He is quite
unconcerned."

I know that voice. It's the voice Mum used to talk to Steven
when he was a baby. Mum has fallen in love.

The baby is taken somewhere else, and I sink to a place just
below the sounds in the room: the scratching, busy sounds
of nurses cleaning up, taking things away; the doctor, telling
Mum in a low voice, as if I were dying, about "a drug to dry up
the milk. It's expensive, but it's very effective." A nurse whispering to another nurse: "Did you hear how much it weighed?
Nine pounds *four.*"

After I am woken and lifted into a wheelchair and wheeled down the hall, I know we are about to pass the nursery. I want to stop. I want to see him again, as if it were Christmas morning; I'm so tired, but I've got a present and I want to play with it . . . I can't say it. My lips don't move fast enough, but my right hand twitches. My wheelchair stops at the nursery doorway. A clear plastic crib is parked there with my baby inside. He sleeps, stretched out like a puppy. He's so real.

I wake up in a room soft with the pre-dawn. A pale light reaches in from down the hallway, and I hear the nursery doors close and open, and nurses snatch a few words to each other. It's lovely. I am content to never move. Let me stay just here and let time stop here in this safe place just before dawn.

But eventually, two nurses come in to check on me. "Can you move much?" When I say no, they tell me not to worry. They'll give me a bath in the room. They find my bag and soap. Soon the air in the room is saturated with the smell of violets. I am all prickles, stitches, and stings, and I seem to be clenched, waiting for reproach. But the women sponge me with warm water and warm voices. They talk to me as if I haven't done anything wrong.

At the door, the head nurse pauses. "Did you . . . do you . . . want to feed the baby? When you can move?"

"Yes," I say. I want to get to know the baby before they take him away. This is why I chose Boothville. Grief is better than shock.

That night, a midwife carries him in against her shoulder. She hands me a small glass bottle about a quarter filled with formula, gives me a few words of instruction, and leaves us alone. I know how to do this. My brother's birth does not seem that long ago. But I like hearing the midwife instruct me. After the bottle, I rub the baby's back gently in a circular motion and tuck him into the bed next to me. He sleeps deeply and easily, wrapped in trust. He has no idea the lady from the adoption service is coming on Thursday. He's as calm as milk.

Last night, someone asked me for a name to write on his card. Out of all the boys' names I know, there is only one I like. Matthew. It has softness in it, and intimacy, and a kind of joy. But I can't give the name Matthew to this baby. It must be reserved for the baby that I keep. I like—or at least don't hate—the name Kristian. I try to make Kristian fit. I want it to settle over his fluffy brown round head. But it won't. Kristians are wispy and blond and Scandinavian. Matthew is the only name for this baby.

A man and a woman emerge from the veranda door at the other side of my room and limp slowly into the room's velvety darkness, into my peace. I get ready to resent them. The woman is wearing a maternity gown and has a huge belly under it, but I can tell she's willowy even though she is stooped with pain. The man, stocky and shorter than her, is holding her upper arm.

"Oh, hello!" the woman says and stops. It's the couple from antenatal class, Jamie and Barbara. Barbara of the clear eyes. "Sorry, we didn't see you there. We're walking through labor."

"Wow. You can *walk?*"

"Yes," Barbara says. "It actually helps."

"Yeah," says Jamie.

"So long as I keep walking," says Barbara. "It seems to—oh, how beautiful!" She's caught sight of Matthew's sleeping face peeping over the blanket.

"Oh, look!" says Jamie.

"Yeah," I say, "but I'm going to give him up."

"Oh, why?" they gasp, together.

"Because I'm going to be a journalist," I say. "I'm going to uni. I'm going to have a career."

"Ohh," says Barbara. "No reason you can't have both."

"No," says Jamie.

"No, I—" I pause. I just haven't thought of it before. "Both? You mean, at once?"

"Yeah," says Barbara. "Why not? There's all sorts of help out there now. You can get single mother's benefit, and you can keep studying, you can go part time."

"I'm already part time," I say. "But I'm not married."

She laughs that breathy laugh again. "Jamie and I aren't married. Jamie and I were a one-night stand! Weren't we, hon? And if you're worried about finances, well, you can always get around finances somehow."

She winces and touches her stomach. "Better keep moving. Think about it, though. You should do it, you should keep him."

Barbara and Jamie walk into the light in the hallway and leave me alone with Matthew. And everything is different.

I stare into a darkness that seems somehow sharper and cleaner than before, and I think. I think of journalism, and time, and if the road we choose into the future has to be a particular shape, and what I might be capable of. And what I might really want.

How Little

Liz Windhorst Harmer

It was not my strength that wanted nursing,
it was my imagination that wanted soothing.
—Joseph Conrad, *Heart of Darkness*, 1899

The books I pack in my hospital birth bags are never the
books I later need to have packed. What I need after birth
is the literary equivalent of a long, tight hug, a whispered
promise that this will pass, that you will be okay. A "feel-
good" story is what I need after my body has been wrenched
open, a baby excised and then tethered to me by invisible
threads. *People* magazine is needed. Perhaps *Us Weekly*. I will
need stories of justice and heroism, winners winning against
impossible odds. Rescued dolphins, happy polar bears. I
will need pictures of beautiful people in sunglasses, pushing
shopping carts filled with kale and coconut water. Nothing
too heavy, nothing too mean. I never believe it beforehand,
but my postpartum needs include a protective circle, even
around the celebrities. Even a whiff of schadenfreude will
bring tears.

Experts say that after birth, a woman and her baby—the skin of one upon the skin of the other—are bathed in oxytocin: the love hormone, the magic potion responsible for sex and families and the maternal instinct. Unfortunately, like all love potions, it makes a person too open and vulnerable, too impressionable to all incoming stimuli. A person who takes a love potion in a fairy tale will fall in love with whomever she sees first, and this love will be binding. A baby monkey who does not have a mother will fall in love with a clothes hanger draped in fur.

When my hormones are finally regulated, perhaps three months in, and I am striding around in the world, all of that seems amusing. When my hormones are bottoming out on that third day postpartum, this bondage of love and its chemical facts are terrifying. Truly horrifying, as though I am staring into the mouth of hell, staring death in its grizzled face, looking at a demon and trying to remember what my mommy looks like.

And every few hours there is a baby I must feed.

In *The Art of Fiction,* John Gardner's famous book on the craft of writing, a strange assertion is made in the final pages, sandwiched between remarks about doing writing exercises. At first they seem elitist:

> The true writer has a great advantage over most
> other people: He knows the great tradition of
> literature, which has always been the cutting edge
> of morality, religion, and politics, to say nothing of

social reform. He knows what the greatest literary
minds are proud to do and will not stoop to.

What do great literary minds *not stoop to?* And how does literary content relate to the "cutting edge of morality"? Have not
all the greats depicted horrors? Even the Bible has rape scenes.

Gardner taught Raymond Carver and Joyce Carol Oates. He
also wrote great, long novels and a book titled *On Moral Fiction*
in which he skewers his contemporaries—John Barth, John
Updike, and Donald Barthelme, among others—and thereby
tarnishes his reputation. It is so unseemly and puritanical to
speak of morals, of abstractions or absolutes like "Truth" and
"Goodness." I know of his writing through my father, who calls
Gardner's novels "moral" without explaining what he means,
beyond the fact that after reading them he feels hope.

In *On Moral Fiction* Gardner suggests that "it is for the
pleasure of exercising the capacity to love that we pick up
a book at all." We sometimes forget how what pleases us
sometimes corresponds to what is good for us, often at this
intersection called love. This may be an answer to why writers write as much as it explains why readers read. It is for the
same pleasure—of exercising the capacity to love—that we
build families, have children.

Of course, sometimes the force of love is no pleasure.

I was smarter in the ignorance of my first pregnancy. I packed
my magazines, temporarily forgetting books, focusing on
motherhood. I cheerily read my fashion advice and celebrity
gossip. I did hit bottom on the fifth day—that thing they call

"baby blues"—and it was not like any blues I'd ever felt. It was more like the grief after a loved one has died. Every time I thought about the life I'd had before motherhood, I burst into tears. I believed I was grieving my former self. I cried when my dog cocked her head at me with what looked like sympathy, and I cried when my husband held the baby so that I could get dressed. When the dog lapped at my husband's glass of juice, I moaned and mourned over it. It had been his favorite juice, and now it was all gone!

Everything seemed lost, everywhere diminished. There was, and would forever be, too little of me. Too little time for each other, too little sleep. But these blues did pass; my hormones regulated.

For a while, it seemed like a good idea not to have any more children.

But twenty-two months later, there we were again, in the hospital, my body torn up and ravaged, nearly too sodden and heavy to walk, and a newborn baby mewling in her bassinet. We had ourselves discharged within twenty-four hours, thinking that getting home sooner might stop the arrival of torrential grief, but we could not outrun it. This time I was reading books again. Literature had been my constant. Except for those weeks surrounding my first daughter's birth, I had read books for company since I was a child and had made books my life as much as I could, so I thought that books, novels, any story well told must be the salve. I read instead of sleeping, which was a big mistake. The grief came and kept me from resting. I was afraid to be alone, lonely for my husband and toddler, afraid to sleep. It is a kind of bottoming out, as they call this hormonal transition. It feels like you have swooned too far too quickly, as on a roller coaster, as to the bottom of a whirlpool, looking up at a wall of water soon to come crashing down.

In the bottom of that bottoming out, I read *Olive Kitteridge* by Elizabeth Strout. It is a beautifully written novel-in-stories, winner of the Pulitzer Prize, and it terrified me. Old age would come, and perhaps it would be lonely like Olive's. Sentences drove themselves like stakes into the loosened soil of my oxytocin-addled brain: "There are worse things than chaos," Olive thinks, looking at her grown son and his young family. *There are worse things than chaos. There are worse things than chaos.* How horrible! There are worse things than this? Than a two-year-old and a baby and a husband, all of whom you love, all of whom you'll never find enough energy and time to properly love?

With falling in love comes, swiftly, the failure of love. This happens to me with each new relationship: I know that I will eventually lose my loved one or be lost. I know that my love will fail, no matter how much I want to honor it. I am too little to prevent the passage of time, the loss of my children to their own lives, the fact that I will hurt them and they me, and, in the end, the death that we will all face.

I read to my children from *Where the Wild Things Are*, haunted by its phrases, too: "We'll eat you up, we love you so." Even something with as little edge as a cuddly Muppet—even our Elmos and our Kermits—seemed warped and frightening in those days of facing my own darkness and my own short-comings. Their cheer was a life raft, and I could see how flimsy it was. A mere puppet, not real. That *Sesame Street* theme song—*su-u-u-nny days*—was about a place I would never again be able to visit.

The grief did not pass that time, not for many months and almost over a year. It grew into the hungry beast of postpartum depression, and I didn't know it until it was almost too late.

More than two years later, I prepared for my third birth and its attendant grief as I had once prepared for labor. I saw a psychiatrist. I took my vitamins and kept up with exercise. I made vows to myself to find sleep. I got sleeping pills. I even encapsulated my placenta because I had been told it could put a dent in postpartum despair. I would spend a few extra days in the hospital to get more rest and to have more people watching over me. I wasn't going to let depression grab me by the throat again. This time I was going to wait for it behind a door with a baseball bat, a trembling woman awaiting an intruder.

I did not think through appropriate reading material as carefully. The novel *Angels* by Denis Johnson sat in my duffel bag, ticking.

I don't believe in censorship. Neither does Gardner. But still, he writes:

> Every writer should be aware that he might be
> read by the desperate, by people who might be
> persuaded toward life or death. It does not mean
> . . . that writers should write moralistically, like
> preachers. And it does not mean that writers
> should lie. It means only that they should think,

always, of what harm they might inadvertently do
and not do it.

What is the writer's responsibility to her readers? Isn't the
writer responsible only to the work? The writer has a responsibility not only to the reader but to telling the truth as she sees
it. Literature must grapple; it must reveal. I want grappling and
revelations, too. I don't believe in literature as distraction.

I don't believe that literature should be an escape—*merely*
escapist, *merely* entertaining—and I do not believe it should
be didactic or moralizing. I read for simpler reasons. For
company. For me, stories have always been a salve against
loneliness, perhaps a crutch. More real than reality. When I
first moved out into my own apartment, homesick and broke,
I watched *Live with Regis and Kelly* and other morning shows
not because I enjoyed the banter but because it kept alive for
me the idea of New York, which, for some reason, I found
soothing. Good novels and stories are like that fake backdrop
of the Manhattan skyline, only more beautiful and less false.

Gardner urges writers to remember that we live in a world
"where teenagers have a chemical propensity toward anguish,
people between their thirties and their forties have a tendency
to get divorced, and people in their seventies have a tendency
toward loneliness, poverty, self-pity, and sometimes anger."
We live in a world in which people are doing difficult things,
facing evil, undergoing hardship, losing loved ones. We live
in a world vulnerable to hormonal shifts. Women who have
just delivered their babies sometimes feel like they have lost
all their cushioning. In that world after birth, it always seems
that the stories I told myself about the meaning of life—that

it *had* meaning, that people were good—were all false, with nothing to replace them.

What would it mean to write with our readers' emotional lives in mind? Perhaps it means only to write as we would want to be read, with forgiveness and with care.

It is not Denis Johnson's fault that I lost two liters of blood after labor and had to have emergency surgery; it is not Johnson's fault that I again teetered at the edge of a chasm, nearly falling in. It is the babies, the hormones, the horrible flux of those careening feelings, yet another thing we must endure after having endured birth itself. The deck is stacked against us: around the third day, after we are sleep-deprived and our milk comes in, so too do the hormones flood us. Before that, there is something like a shift change: the hockey team abandoning the rink to tag in the alternates. For the span of that transition, after the old hormones have gone away but before the new ones are there to replace them, the net is undefended.

This time, the grief came in the span of a moment. My midwife asked me, "Are you feeling good?"

"Oh, yes," I said. "I think I am, actually. Maybe the placenta worked."

She left the room to answer a call, and when she returned, I was bawling.

Since becoming a mother, I have realized what it means to be a woman. I don't mean physically, of course. It's only that my body had not been limited in this way before. I had never been so vulnerable. I had gone striding around the world exactly like a man, never in need of protection. Now it seems to me that the world is not divided by lines of gender—not by sex organs or by performances of masculinity and femininity—but only by hormones. The hormones that make us vulnerable versus the hormones that make us offend. With a baby, that embodiment of loneliness and vulnerability, comes horror at the possibility that you cannot be trusted with her. You are not enough to protect her. The world is too big and too vicious and you are too little. You need a world in which the men set out lifeboats and say "Women and children first." Even if it goes against everything you believe.

After that third birth, the night after my hormones left me defenseless, I lay in my bed, baby asleep nearby, the IV tower releasing blood into my body by little clicks and sighs. I pulled in a breath, yoga-style, and tried to push it calmly through the rivers of my body. Tears came trembling to my lips and nose, but I forced them away. Bad habit would not beget bad feeling. I picked up Denis Johnson's first novel with my unencumbered hand. I began to read.

If you've read Johnson, you'll know that the prose is extraordinary: it is beautifully rendered, with images that startle you with their originality, daring sentences with an edge of cruelty. They are like glittering knives. An example: "She stared with hatred at [her daughter's] closed eyes and soon realized the child had fallen asleep. The weightlessness of fear replaced the weight of anger as the bus sailed down the gullet the headlights made." *The gullet the headlights made*—what an image. You feel yourself hurtling; it puts the reader in motion. Another: "The four motels of Jamie's experience had all been flat. They hadn't stood up to declare themselves for six stories amid congested Pittsburgh, they had only reclined by their swimming pools taking the dust off the cars going by." The sentences work hard against cliché.

Angels features a broke (and broken) young woman who is traveling by bus across the country with her baby and toddler. As I read, my throat dried up. I became frightened as I closed my eyes to go to sleep, almost paranoid in my thinking. I could hear voices outside my hospital room, someone shouting into a phone in a foreign language, and I hugged my blanket to myself, fearing the sort of thing that was about to befall Johnson's character. Someone was about to slip her drugs. Someone was going to rape and knife her. Eventually, she would come down from whatever high and hazily realize that she didn't know the person looking after her children.

> She was on her back with her hands cuffed behind her, her knees locked under her chin by the ongoing adrenaline convulsion of fear. Peripherally she understood that nobody human was messing with her like this, but something much more dangerous, a dark configuration of people and events, something original, something about to be named.

I closed the book after this rape scene. The scene in which one rapist exclaims about how beautiful it is while the other suggests they do "something" with a knife.

Parenting can be bleak. To do it, we need beliefs to buoy us. For example: *No matter what happens your children will be okay.* For example: *Everything will be okay as long as you love them.*

Geoff Dyer writes that central to "Johnson's dramatized worldview is the belief that it is the mangled and damaged, the downtrodden, who are in the best place to achieve—*withstand* is probably a better verb—enlightenment."

Oh, let Johnson be wrong. It goes against all of my better judgments of taste and politics to recommend that anyone stay away from any books. But some allowances must be made for vulnerability. Sometimes, as the psalmist says, your soul is like a weaned child within you. Avoid *Angels* until you are large enough to withstand it.

As for me, I still do not know how the story turns out. I am afraid that it will reignite that grief and horror, as though the pages themselves are loaded with toxins. I turned instead to a novel by John Gardner. In the valley of postpartum hormones, I trusted only Gardner not to frighten me with the awful truth of the world. I read his long novel *Mickelsson's Ghosts,* which, despite some dark and difficult content, did not disturb me. Things do not end up all right, exactly, but it's true: you will be okay. This too shall pass, and you are never, never alone.

Becoming His Mother

Mary A. Scherf

A mother is her baby's first interpreter. She explains the world. She tells her children who they are. My mother's words marked my life with guilt and doubt. She said, "You should be ashamed of yourself," and I flushed and wanted to disappear. She told the nun who called to ask if my outspoken restlessness might indicate a problem, "No. She just doesn't know how to keep her mouth shut." When she said, "Your father and I didn't know how lucky we were when we didn't have children," I understood that my disobedience was the reason for her unhappiness.

My mother, my first mirror, reflected only disappointment until I learned to look away. She mocked my dreams, smacked my head. The last time she hit me, I was twenty-one and due to marry two weeks later. When, at thirty, I left that husband, my mother said, "Who gave you the idea you should be happy in this life? That's what heaven's for."

By then, I wasn't listening. I'd finally decided to stop waiting for the next life and start living in this one.

Infertility overshadowed my second, happier marriage. When we decided to adopt, the remembered hum of my mother's dissatisfaction grew loud in my head, clashing with the voice in my heart urging me forward. I wanted to be a good mother, better than my own. We chose a boy. There was less risk with a son that the past would trap me, less chance I would confuse him with my childhood self or my angry, frightened mother or my domineering grandmother—the unhappy women clawing at me like crabs in a steamer as I scrabbled past, seeking air and light.

This was the plan when I boarded the plane to Guatemala City to bring Luis home.

Humid air rolls through the cab, smelling of diesel and exhaust. The streets are mottled with evening shadows. From the back seat, I can feel the cab's engine idling when we stop. The tiny fists of street children crowd the open window beside me, clutching tight red buds already bending toward death. Brown eyes watch me from beneath tangled black hair. High-pitched voices seek something in a language I can't understand. The children are far too young to be wandering through traffic on darkening streets.

I lean forward in my seat so the driver can hear me through the clouded plexiglass that separates us. "What are they saying?"

"They want to sell you the roses."

I begin fumbling for my wallet.

"Ignore them," he says. His tone stops me, the reprimand clear.

The light changes and the cab lurches forward. The children barely have time to snatch their arms back. I want to save them all, but I may already be too late to claim even Luis.

Almost a week has passed since the adoption agency's urgent call summoning us to assume custody of our child two months early. The Guatemalan police have begun raiding foster homes in a doomed attempt to stall much-needed reforms to the country's adoption system. Some of the waiting babies are being transferred to orphanages; others are returning temporarily to their birth mothers. We can't pack up and go on the day we get the call; the immigration paperwork isn't finished, and the small legal-services project I run needs to be readied for my absence. Steve, my husband, stays behind to fast-track the documents we need to bring Luis home. My arrival is four days past the agency's deadline.

The cab drops me at the Hotel Casa Grande late Sunday evening. I register with the lone clerk in a seemingly deserted lobby. The stress of the trip fires up my anxieties. This adoption will fail because of my delay. Luis will grow up in an orphanage or be lost to the streets like the little flower sellers by the highway. Either way, I will bear the blame for his ruin.

My room, at the end of a dim hallway next to the hotel kitchen, is worn, almost seedy. I heave two large suitcases onto the bed and begin untangling myself from the straps of the smaller bags slung across my shoulders. A furtive tap at the door makes me jump. I open it only as far as the brass chain will allow. A slender woman with tired eyes stands on the other side of the flimsy barrier. Her shoulders slump forward with the weight of the drowsy baby in her arms.

"I'm Lillian," the woman says. "I work with Rosa." Rosa is our Guatemalan adoption lawyer. I open the door.

Lillian's face, just visible above the top of the baby's head, is pale. Her expression echoes my fatigue and worry.

"I knew it was you," she says, tilting her head toward the umbrella stroller strapped to my luggage, "so I followed you. I didn't want to give you the baby in the lobby. Here he is."

She hands Luis to me without ceremony, puts his few belongings on the bed.

"He has diarrhea," she says. "He'll need to see a pediatrician right away." She speaks as if she is reciting a list from memory. Working quickly while she talks, she pulls a can of powdered formula out of a bag and shows me how to mix his bottles. "Call Rosa in the morning. She'll bring the adoption papers tomorrow."

"Wait," I say. "What doctor should he see?"

She is already out the door. "Rosa will give you a name when you call her," she says without turning back.

Luis squirms and slides lower in my arms. I hike him up and feel the heat rising from his sturdy body. He smells faintly of cornstarch and bleach.

This is how my first son comes to me.

I began thinking about being a mother the year I turned seven, after my brother was born and I was no longer the baby of the family. My docile dolls bored me, but Ray didn't. He was always in motion, lips pursing, fingers grasping, legs pedaling. Even asleep, he held my rapt attention. The gentle pulsing of his fontanel was proof of his life unfolding, separate from mine. Motherhood seemed wondrous.

I was not the only one affected by his arrival. A baby can strain and change everyone in a family.

My father used to sing my sister Diane and me to sleep. Crouched between our twin beds, he crooned "Toyland" and "Daddy's Little Girl." In those moments, it was easy to imagine I was his star as I drifted into sleep. Then, one Sunday night

during the winter Ray was an infant, something in my father
snapped. The ride home from my grandparents' seemed longer
than the hour it took. Perhaps I was too hot or too itchy, both
common complaints. Perhaps we left too soon after eating
and I felt carsick. My father told me to be quiet. I whined and
whined, and when he told me to shut up, I didn't.

When we got home, my father dragged me from the back
seat of the car and whacked me several times, harder than I'd
ever been hit by either of my parents. He paused to unlock
the back door of our row house so my sister and my mother,
holding baby Ray, could get out of the cold. I hurried in the
door behind them, but he wasn't done with me yet. He hit me
again and again while I yelled for him to stop and struggled
to escape his grip. I broke free, ran the two flights up to the
bedroom I shared with my sister, slammed the door, and hid in
our closet.

He didn't follow. My mother found me cowering on the
floor among the shoes. She took off my wool coat and matching snow pants, and then lifted my skirt and petticoat. Under
all those layers, my thigh was bright red from the beating.
Ever after, my father told me what happened that night was my
fault. "You brought out the worst in people," he said. When I
was seven, I believed him.

The following spring, the time came for me to make my
first communion. Over the winter, I had become too fat to
wear my older sister's hand-me-down dress. My grandmother
was making a rare weekday visit to fit me for a new one. The
weather was warm, and my mother, with Ray in his coach, met
my sister and me after school. She mistakenly thought there
would be enough time for us to walk to the town library before

her mother arrived. That afternoon, I discovered a biography of Amelia Earhart. The fact that women could fly planes astonished me. I read all the way home, lagging further and further behind my family.

We came in by the basement door and found my grandmother sitting in a chair by the front door with the dress in her lap. She frowned, her eyes narrowing with a barely contained anger. We had kept her waiting, me longest of all. My fingers flew over buttons and zippers. My navy-blue uniform fell around my ankles as my grandmother yanked white eyelet over my head. She prodded and pinned while my mother fluttered around us nervously, like her parakeet did when anyone got close to his cage. I recognized my mother's reaction, so like my own when I displeased her. She was afraid of her mother, too. It was a pattern, repeating itself.

As I stood between them, absorbing their anger and their fear, I began to wonder. If I became a mother, would the pattern be the same? Or could I change it? Amelia Earhart was a different kind of woman, one who was brave and learned to fly. Maybe when I grew up, I could be different, too, and my life wouldn't be the same as my mother's. Maybe a child of mine would not have to be afraid.

I began to look outside my family for the lessons I needed. The Sunday school teacher I helped, a young mother with a shy, toothy smile and a pillbox hat, was quietly attentive to her daughters and the other preschoolers. I imitated her gentleness and drew the youngest children to me. Next-door neighbors showed me the creativity in homemaking and the pleasures of fresh-baked bread and homemade applesauce. An affectionate couple around the corner trusted me to babysit their growing family twice a week for four years. The arrival of each child increased the love in their marriage rather than diluting it.

As he got older, my brother offered me the chance to practice what I learned. I entertained him in his playpen and on the living-room floor. He introduced me to the world of dinosaurs. We hunted crayfish together. On summer evenings, I pushed his swing until the fireflies drifted up like embers from the tall grass in the park.

This new experience of love opened my heart and made me more compassionate. As I changed, I wanted my mother to change, too. But she held tightly to the strict ways she had learned from her mother, demanding obedience, expecting disappointment, fearing anything new. A poem I wrote was published in the local paper. She snorted at my impracticality and told me I'd better marry a rich man. When my interest shifted to being a lawyer, she said I should be a legal secretary instead. If I learned to type, I would never starve. In opposing her, I became as stubborn and rigid as she was. Her control over me was weakening, yet she continued to hit me, as if violent force would keep me in line. My tears made her angrier, so I locked myself in the bathroom and buried my face in a towel when I cried.

I wanted to rest in my mother's love as if it was a hammock holding me, soft and taut at the same time. Instead, there was only a stone-hard place. What she did wasn't right, but I loved her and needed to believe that she loved me. I convinced myself that I deserved the physical discipline. Eventually I would learn to trust my instincts and see clearly what was good in myself and others. But throughout my teens and twenties, the effort to accept her distorted notion of love skewed my perceptions, confused my relationships. I experienced competing impulses toward love and self-protection, which left me isolated, numb, unable to act.

Alone in the hotel room, holding Luis in my arms, long-forgotten doubts immobilize my good intentions. My heart goes blank. All I know about caring for a baby is temporarily forgotten. His arrival feels sordid, like he has come to me as contraband, part of some back-alley deal. I take a deep breath and steady my heart. I lay Luis on the bed and begin to undress him. From beneath an embroidered bonnet, a blue sweater, a white dress shirt and a tiny, buttoned undershirt, the child I have chosen emerges. I am as ready to be his mother as I'll ever be. My heart leaps, pinwheeling into love for him with no restraints. I hope all I have will be enough.

We muddle through the first few days and nights. I sterilize bottles in the tiny bathroom sink and eventually move us from the hotel basement to a large, sunny room on the second floor. I find a doctor who overlooks the absence of documents and treats his fever, pronounces him healthy. The promised adoption papers remain elusive. I carry the constant fear that our tenuous relationship will be exposed. The presence of armed soldiers on the sidewalks in front of the hotel feeds my unease. Despite the difficulties, Luis and I grow used to each other. I pay attention. He communicates what he needs and I respond. Caring for him is that simple.

Late on Wednesday afternoon, Rosa brings Estella, Luis's mother, to meet me. I am barely five-foot-two, and still I tower over her tiny figure. Her face is broad like her son's, but her skin is ruddy in contrast to his. Her black hair hangs to her waist in a single thick braid. She wears a plain white blouse and a bright skirt woven in horizontal stripes of green, black, pink, and yellow. Luis smiles when he sees her. I place him in her arms. Before long, he begins to fuss and reaches for me. My heart beats faster when she hands him back, but there is no time to savor his choice. When I look up from his face, Estella is crying.

She begins to speak softly and Rosa translates. She says she loves Luis, but she has no money to support him. I cry, too, and say I will tell him about her love. I promise to care for Luis as well as I can and show her a picture of Steve and me so she knows what his new father looks like. I hope she can see that we are a happy couple. Estella studies the picture, nods, and turns away to speak to Rosa in private.

"She has given you her blessing," Rosa says. "She will come back to my office now and sign temporary custody papers."

I am awake for hours after the women leave. Before I came to Guatemala, I thought only about the babies who needed homes. Their mothers remained an abstract notion. When the agency steered us to Guatemala, we accepted their one-page summary of the program without asking many questions. I wanted the quick and convenient process that they promised. Grinding poverty seemed inevitable in Central America. I didn't consider the impact of a decades-long war or the allegations of government atrocities against the Guatemalan people.

Meeting Estella, hearing her story, has made her as real to me as her son, flesh and bone and heart. Her love for him is undeniable. I cannot ignore the fact that the money we are spending on adoption fees and travel expenses would be enough, in her hands, to raise Luis herself. The bargain we have struck becomes unimaginable. My desire to be a mother will be fulfilled because she has renounced hers.

Who am I to ask this mother to give up her child?

On our sixth day together, when I wake up, Luis is watching me through the bars of his crib, brown eyes bright and focused above a wide, toothless grin. My heart expands like a flower blooming in a time-lapsed film. I see myself reflected in his eyes—recognized, worthy, claimed. I imagine him thinking, *Why not? Let's do this. You and me.*

I lean on my elbow to watch him. His attention returns to the task of studying how his body works. He holds his wrists above his face and rotates them. He swings his right leg across his body, tries to roll towards me, and smiles again. We are forging a connection. There is room for joy today. I have papers to prove he is legally in my custody. My son is healthy. He has the right formula now, the right shampoo for his cradle cap. He is safe, and he is mine.

I mix a new bottle, sterilize the rest, sort the clothes that came back from the laundry, and settle him on my lap to feed. He falls asleep in my arms. I have no desire to move. There are no more worried calls to make. There is nothing left to do but love my son. I sniff his downy head, inhaling the scent of baby shampoo, talcum powder, and his own milky-sweet smell. His warm body rests solidly against me, anchoring me at last. I vow this baby will know that he is wanted and loved.

Hours later, I am called to the hotel lobby. Estella is back. From the top of the stairs, I see her below me, sitting on the sofa, surrounded by three somber men and another woman. I descend slowly with Luis in my arms, afraid that she has come with family or members of her church to say she's changed her mind. Despite how much I love him, I know by the time I reach the bottom step that if she asks for his return, I will honor her request.

Instead, I am arrested.

Estella claims I stole Luis from her at a bus stop. My legal training does not help me here. I cannot represent myself, I do not speak the language, and the courts aren't open on Friday afternoons. Before I am taken away, I insist on retrieving my passport and packing a bag of bottles and diapers for Luis. I give the arresting officer my only copy of the custody papers. Somewhere between leaving the hotel and arriving at police headquarters, the papers disappear. I plan to call Rosa, our lawyer, when I get to the station, but she is already there; she has been arrested, too.

I spend three days in Santa Teresa, the women's prison. Concrete bunks, cold showers, meals served from buckets twice a day. I can't force myself to eat. Inmates with knife-slashed faces stroke my arms, my hair, and declare their love for me, *la pobrecita blanca*. I endure the absence of Luis. The sorrow cuts so deep, sometimes I can't breathe.

There is too much time to think. On Sunday afternoon, a spool of painful memories unwinds while I pass the time in the prison courtyard. The recollection of one failure bleeds into the next. Scenes from the end of my first marriage replay in my head. He waits for me at the train station in the morning, says he hates me, runs away. In the marriage counselor's office, I sit with my trench coat balled up in my lap; his legs are crossed, one foot kicking the air. The therapist urges us to reveal what we need from each other. Irate, my husband blurts: "She's not supposed to need anything."

Then his angry prediction, during one of our last arguments: "If you leave me, you'll never have a child. You know that, don't you? Never."

The backward spiral ends where it always does, with memories of my mother. All the angry voices begin to sound like hers, assigning blame, passing judgment. "This is what you get for trying to be happy."

I sit on the wall with my darkest memories strewn about like salvage from a wreck. There is no escape—from Santa Teresa or the prison of my thoughts. An inner darkness overtakes me. I give in to the babble of shame and guilt; within moments of surrender they are gone, taking my mother's voice with them. In the silence that remains, I find a measure of peace.

In this place, finally, I know that I am enough.

My release, when it is arranged, is conditional. I am not allowed to leave the country without *libertad simple;* I can't get simple liberty until Estella withdraws her complaint. Embassy investigators search for days before they find Estella and bring her back to the capital. She confirms that I did not steal Luis. She gave him up voluntarily. When the police began raiding foster homes, the agency sent Luis back to her for a few days. Their brief reunion gave Estella the idea that she could change her mind. She cooperated with the police in the hope of reclaiming her son.

During her interview with the investigators, Estella agrees
to withdraw her complaint and allow the adoption to continue.
I begin to imagine Luis in my arms again. Then she makes her
sworn statement and has another change of heart. She retracts
the accusations, but when she is asked if the adoption can be
completed, Estella says, "No."

Estella doesn't understand the impact of that one word.
Without her consent, I cannot complete the adoption, but she
cannot take Luis home. Her parental rights were terminated
at an earlier stage of the adoption proceedings. Luis belongs to
Guatemala now. He is sent to an orphanage. I go home alone.

In the days following my return, I go through the motions of
resuming my former life, but I no longer fully inhabit my body.
Part of me watches the days go by from behind an invisible
barrier that muffles all my senses. People flock around me to
ask what prison was like. Inside, I duck and turn away from
them. My public shell deflects their curiosity with flip comments. "It was nothing like *Midnight Express*," I say, referring
to a dark movie about an American jailed in a Turkish prison
on drug charges. "More like a third-rate Girl Scout camp."

No one asks about Luis.

A few weeks pass. I walk up Oxford Avenue from the
Margaret-Orthodox El stop, lugging home a briefcase full of
papers I will ignore again tonight. Work has long been my ref-
uge, but it has lost the power to distract me. The emptiness of
my arms stops me right there on the street. The pain of Luis's
physical absence, of being unmoored from his small weight,
stabs my chest, sharp and hot. I drop my bag on the sidewalk

and close my eyes. I don't care who sees me. I breathe deeply, waiting for the feeling to pass, but the memory of how it felt to hold him persists. I open my eyes again and place my right hand around the silver pylon of the street light nearby, just to feel something real beneath my palm. The cool metal soothes me. As quickly as the pain rose, it subsides, and I plod home in the dimming light of a late October evening.

The call comes one month later. I am at my desk reviewing client files. A social worker introduces herself. She works in the domestic infant program at the agency that arranged our failed adoption of Luis. It has been three years since we began to work with them; I had forgotten our names were also on the infant list.

"A baby was born last week," she says. She names a hospital ten minutes from our home in Philadelphia. "There are questions about his health, and his grandmother can't take on a newborn. His mother signed the papers to begin an adoption when he was a day old. He'll be ready for release soon and he needs a home. Are you interested?"

After Guatemala, Steve and I told each other we would not adopt again. We were finished taking risks. We had nieces and nephews to indulge. But loving Luis had opened my heart; and losing him had made me strong. I can take another chance because I know I will survive.

When I call him, Steve says, "I will if you will." The excitement in his voice raises the hair on my arms.

"Yes," I say. I am calm, steady; my answer is clear. It has nothing to do with what I used to tangle up with the longing to have a baby—the need to feel whole or loved or worthy of motherhood. Prison has distilled my maternal desire to its essence. I say yes because I'm ready to love this baby on his own terms.

Michael comes to us straight from the hospital when he is sixteen days old. He is barefoot, wrapped in a blanket, wearing shorts on the last day of November. He weighs six pounds, has long fingers, long toes, pale, skinny legs that constantly work free of the covers, hair the color of a tarnished penny. The antibiotic drip he needed during his first week of life has scarred the backs of his hands. He is too fragile for his mother, as she is for him. She does not change her mind.

The first night, everything I do for him feels unfamiliar. Lack of sleep disorients me. At four in the morning, he drinks a bottle in greedy gulps. There is no trace of Luis's placid nature and easy rhythm. When I change him afterward, he arches his back without warning. In a stiff-limbed spasm, he flips off the bureau. I crouch, knees banging against the bottom drawer, and catch him as he falls.

On a cold January morning when he is eight weeks old, Michael sits in a denim bouncy chair on the kitchen table while I clear away breakfast. His weight has doubled and he stays awake longer each day. He kicks off the blanket again. When I lean over to tuck him in, he opens his blue eyes and stares at me.

"I see you," I say, smiling.

His eyes widen, as if he recognizes me, too.

Blue Pools

Anastasia Rubis

I had visualized my baby in yoga class.

"Imagine your fetus with every characteristic you wish it to have," Swami Satchishankara coached nine women with basketball bellies, all lying in *sabasana*. I had picked intelligence, happiness, and humor—and pictured a dazzling, photogenic grin.

But Kassandra did not have Aegean eyes and sun-streaked hair as I had imagined. Instead, forty-eight hours after her delivery at Lenox Hill, she bore an alarming resemblance to my mother-in-law. *Surely babies change*, I worried. She couldn't have inherited *all* of her genes from that side of the family.

I stared at the eight-pound mammal feeding from what should officially be renamed the umbilical cord to my soul. This is what breasts are for, I realized, though yesterday my sudden C-cups had been noncompliant. Kassandra had not been able to latch on. It was like trying to French-kiss a missile.

Then this morning, the miracle of letdown happened after I frantically dialed La Leche League's hotline and was instructed to take a hot shower. Kassandra's eyes locked on mine as she guzzled. They occupied a huge percentage of her face, and the look inside them was sage and deep. She appeared watchful, serious. She might be a financial analyst, a psychiatrist. Her irises were typical slate, but the rims were emerging turquoise, heading toward blue, it seemed, though everyone warned, "Eye color can change, even after six months."

Don't change, I pleaded. *I have found you in blue pools; you'll be some other person in brown or hazel. Don't leave me now, Kassandra.* The name sounded big. I felt like an impostor saying it. Had we chosen the wrong one?

After getting her fill, the tiny mammal drifted off to sleep, brow easy, lips parted to release my nipple and remaining wide with wonder. We were lying in bed, a position that had the distinct advantage of not being excruciating to my bottom. "Your hemorrhoids will take longer to heal than the episiotomy," Dr. Roth had casually mentioned. The rubber "donut" purchased with high hopes from the drugstore did nothing to dispel the sensation that I was sitting on shards of glass. I was in pain, and nursing left me as parched as if I had swallowed sand. I licked my lips, eyeballing the glass of water perched on the nightstand. *Yikes! What was that?* A shadow darted over the rim of the glass.

I lifted my head and gasped. A cockroach stared back, twitching its evil antennae. My hands flew to Kassandra's face. There hadn't been a cockroach in this apartment since John and I moved in four years ago, but now one had decided to appear six inches from my shiny new germ-free daughter.

"John!"

I could hear the grandparents clucking in the living room, behind the flimsy sheetrock. John tiptoed into the bedroom.

"Did you sleep?" he asked nervously, the way he asked everything these days.

"Look!" I pointed to the glass.

"Aagh!"

"Get it out!"

"Okay, okay." He fumbled. "Let me get a bag."

"Don't let anyone see!"

John slunk to the door, where he crashed headlong into my mother. Clumsily, he backtracked to block the roach, crossing his arms and leaning against the nightstand.

"She's sleeping," I whispered.

"Good," my mother whispered back. "How about a bagel with feta, *koukla*?"

She had spent the night on the pull-out sofa, teaching us to diaper Kassandra's rose-speckled bottom with her expert, gnarled hands. Neither John nor I wanted her to leave. Ever.

At sixty, my mother was still a natural beauty, with green eyes and five gray hairs. She eschewed makeup and favored earth colors for her long, chaste skirts, the kind my sisters and I had loved hanging on to. She was a woman who could raise armies of children, I had the sudden epiphany, because she was egoless and unburdened by the need to constantly improve herself. She was, in truth, a little spaced out, a marvelous attribute in bringing up bunches of kids. Parthena could let things go, which she did, all the time. Earlier, for instance, when I taxed my remaining mental faculties to scrawl a shopping list, she cheerfully forgot it at home. Thus, two hours at the supermarket and still no stool softener.

"I'm not hungry, Ma," I lied.

"Thirsty?" She moved toward the infested glass.

"Wait!" John sprang forward. "Parthena, sure you can't stay an extra night? How about moving in?"

She laughed, diverted from the glass. "I'm going to church to thank God for this healthy baby. But I can come back the next day—"

"That's okay, Mom, I know you don't like driving in." I hated to impose. Besides, she and John had engaged in a snoring contest the previous night, leaving me to pace the dark alone, panicked about Kassandra's next feeding.

My mother was fingering a mysterious object in her blazer pocket and placed it now on the bureau. A lump rose in my throat as I glimpsed the framed photo of my father crossing the finish line of the New York Marathon. I recognized the muddled pain on his features from my own recent reflection in the mirror. I swallowed hard. I would never forgive him. There were two kinds of people in the world: those who made you feel better by their sheer presence and everybody else. George Rubis had left me here with everybody else. He would have bounded into this dark, stuffy apartment with tulips. He would have said, "Let's go get some fresh air," and corralled me and the baby and baby carriage into the September sunshine in minutes.

"She's awake." My mother lit up.

"I need to switch breasts," I said, doing my best not to flinch as Little One suctioned onto my cracked nipple.

A tsunami of perfume hit my nostrils. I jerked the sheet to my chest just as John's mother click-clacked into the bedroom.

Beba Petropoulos was dripping in her Sunday best: faux Chanel suit, gold rope chains, frosted lipstick, and half a bottle of Opium.

"You ate my soup? Is good for your milk," Beba said, averting her eyes from how milk actually got piped into the baby.

"I had two bowls," I said grudgingly. "It was good." Mrs. Petropoulos, Beba, *Mom*. After four years of marriage, I still could not name her.

"First I cut off the chicken's behind, where is poopoo. Then I boil and skim the dirty foam," Beba recited. I'd heard the recipe twenty-seven times but was never going to give her the satisfaction of writing it down.

Through the bedroom wall, I had eavesdropped on my mother and mother-in-law subtly competing over who had brought the most nutritious goodies for me. The Greeks have a word for a woman who has just given life. The *lehona* must eat and rest. It's the only time she can put her feet up and be served.

"Is safe for a baby, this neighborhood?" Beba always addressed her super-erudite comments to me, never John, even when he was standing in the room.

"The neighborhood's safe," I said.

"Babies, they need grass," she said.

You could use some grass, too, lady.

"Maybe Stacy should rest," John finally intervened. He was maneuvering around the cockroach like a football tackle, hunched in a way that gave him breasts—or was I seeing breasts everywhere?

He was handsome, my John. I preferred his brown hair flopping boyishly over his forehead, like today, rather than slicked back to impersonate a wealthy European, as he wore it for the office. John was slow and steady, a tortoise to my hare. He was masculine without being macho and spent a good amount of effort hiding a gentle heart. Mercifully, he had a wicked sense of humor, as good as any comedian's. He needed it, with his parents.

John was supposed to be a doctor by order of the Hippocratic Oath, which dictates (between the lines) that a Greek son shall follow in his father's footsteps. Sophomore year, when John got massacred by organic chemistry and broke the news that he would not be carrying forth the family legacy, his father peeled himself off the floor and ordered John to pick another licensed profession. Art was out. So was business, or else he would take John's American Express card away. John chose architecture, the path of Iktinos and Kallikrates, designers of the Parthenon: the path of least resistance.

"Bravo, look at her eat." My mother beamed.

"You supposed to feed her while she sleeping?" Beba frowned.

"She's not sleeping," I said sharply.

"Oh! She choking!" Beba flailed her arms at the baby's double-gulp.

I rolled my eyes. How I longed for a mother-in-law who ate tuna on rye and read the *New Yorker*.

"Manolis, you supposed to feed the baby while she sleeping?" The doctor's wife deferred to the doctor, who'd been summoned to the doorway by her siren.

I glared at my mother for help. The saint was letting it go, as usual.

"Is not preferred. But as long as . . . *she* burps her afterward." Dr. Petropoulos blanked out on my name. "You using a loofah on your breasts?"

"Loofah?" I winced.

"You want to offer a clean breast. And supplement with cereal, because breastfed babies, ha-ha-ha," he gave his condescending chuckle, "they are anemic."

My blood boiled. What made him an expert in OB/GYN and pediatrics? The big know-it-all trained in urology in communist Romania. He had insisted I should shave my pubic hair before delivery. "More sterile for the baby." He had even contested my due date, embarrassing me at Sunday dinner. "When your last period was?" he asked, scribbling calculations on his napkin.

Now Dr. Petropoulos pinned me with his sullen gaze. "You want me to check your hemorrhoids?"

"Not now." My eyes shot to John, but he was doing what he did best with his parents—not listening. He was not going to save me.

"It's up to you. I can prescribe a cream," Dr. Petropoulos said. "Because if you get an infection, ha-ha-ha, people die of complications."

I considered the dire consequences of abstaining from medical attention. I couldn't leave my girl motherless. I had to make it to her graduation and wedding at all costs.

"Fine. Give me a minute." I didn't know which was more humiliating, needing my father-in-law or having him poke around down there.

Dr. and Mrs. Petropoulos shared the delusion that they breathed a more rarefied air than the rest of society, that they in fact *were* society. I felt virtuous just inviting them to meet their grandchild, after the way they protested when John and I first dated. *Se xemialiase*, they ranted to their prized only son. *She has de-brained you*. I, frankly, was accustomed to approval. By all accounts, I was a good Greek girl—I knew how to set the table for twenty and dust *flokati* rugs off the back porch. I was a good American girl, too, with an Ivy League degree and

a six-figure salary. *What else did they want?* My family and
friends threw up their hands.

What the Petropouloses wanted was an M.D. for a son,
which they were not getting. And to handpick his dumb, pli-
able bride from their approved doctors' circle, which they also
were not getting.

At the prospect of a hemorrhoidal exam, all grandparents
cleared the room. John spun around to inspect the nightstand—
the roach was still glued to the glass. *Phew,* he wiped his brow,
going for levity. I turned my back, cradling my daughter.

Why me? I sank, sank, sank to the bottom of the ocean.
Between the piles, the in-laws, the white-box rental furnished
in college mishmash, and THE COCKROACH, I was not as
elated as a new mother was supposed to be. I had skipped over
the chapter on postpartum depression in *What to Expect When
You're Expecting*. It would never happen to me. I had been
blissful throughout pregnancy, having finally convinced John
to share some propagating material. "Nothing will change," I
said. "We'll never leave the city. I've socked a nest egg away." At
thirty-six, I had outfoxed my weak ovarian reserve. I was going
to be a mommy and achieve every woman's dream.

Now, nine months later, I could only assume it was my
mistakes coming home to roost—the decision to major in
semiotics, to rent and not buy, to try bangs—that prompted
this derangement, despair, despondency, all the "d" words.
I was cut off, buried beneath the layer of earth where people
laughed and clinked glasses and celebrated.

My eyes narrowed at John. I considered myself magnani-
mous for keeping the *why me?* to myself. I hated this room and
my life and it was all his fault.

"I haven't smoked in forty-eight hours," John said.

"Call the press."

John hung his head. "I'll go get something for the . . . insect."

As he opened the door, I heard again the CNN headline
that had been blaring every half hour: John F. Kennedy Jr.
had married in a secret ceremony on some WASPy island no
immigrant's kid had ever heard of. The same day I gave birth,
Camelot welcomed a new princess. And she had quite the bod,
according to the one official photo, in which John was kissing
her hand and she was glowing in a shimmering slip dress.

JFK Jr., sexiest man alive. I had watched those muscles grow
up at Brown while we swam in adjacent lanes at the sports
center on Hope Street. Some days, I hung around the atrium to
admire him on the Nautilus.

Once, at a graduation party off campus, John Kennedy
had tripped over me on his way to the fridge for a beer.
He gripped my shoulders to steady himself, and we looked
into each other's eyes longer than we needed before draw-
ing bashfully away. I was on the verge of blurting that I, too,
summered on a Greek isle (if "summering" included Yiayia's
outhouse), and that my mother had saved the *Life* magazine
with the picture of him saluting his father's casket. But he
was too famous.

Ten minutes later, it was my turn to trip over him on my
way to the bathroom. I overheard him describing Santorini
(a sign!) to some guys, calling it the "lost island of Atlantis,"
just before my feet got tangled in the rug. He flashed a grin
of complicity and offered me his arm, but I waved him off
and barricaded the door. Often, when opportunity knocked,
I pretended not to be home.

After graduation, I ran into him at an alumni event in the city. I was buzzed after two margaritas and bopping around the dance floor.

"Wanna dance?" I tossed out, temporarily bold.

"I've got bad knees," JFK Jr. said but began swaying next to me. The song ended and he kissed me. No. I sailed away and began dancing with another boy. When I looked back, he was gone.

He phoned the next day, I think. My dad took a message that "John called," and I didn't know any other Johns then. But he never called back, and now he had married a princess.

Knock knock. John the husband entered with trepidation. *I have saddled myself with a mere mortal*, I fumed. He gingerly lifted the glass—roach, water, and all—and stuffed it into a plastic bag, tying a knot.

"I'll call Milosh and ask him to spray," he said.

"We can't spray with the baby! It's poisonous!"

"Anyway, I doubt there will be more."

"You doubt? Did you see how close that thing came to her face?"

"What do you want me to do, Stacy?"

"I want there *not* to be a cockroach on my glass when I've just given birth, that's what I want."

Silence.

"Let me get rid of this." John ducked out with the bag.

I should have married Andrew Leftaras, the boring TV weatherman. On our first date, he had pulled out fabric swatches for his Park Avenue Classic Six. On the second, he drove me to his East Hampton beach house. So what if he wore makeup?

Andrew Leftaras's wife surely did not have pests swarming her nightstand when she gave birth to twins. I pictured Vicky Leftaras, salesgirl from Queens, plumped up on pillows, surrounded by Tiffany boxes of baubles her husband lavished upon her for bringing Leftarases into the world.

John was absent for the lesson on buying your wife a gift after she extrudes eight pounds of your DNA. He left the hospital after witnessing the miracle of birth and went home to play guitar. He cried, he confessed. Joy and, okay, feeling a tad overwhelmed. What he didn't have to say, because I knew, was that he was mourning the end of an era: Aegean isles, Swedish girls, summer afternoons. Now there were just diapers and dwindling bank accounts and roaches.

I stared out the window at the flashing red antenna of the World Trade Center. Night was falling. Soon the in-laws would leave, and my mother with them. My heart raced. I had a newborn in the crook of my arm and a husband in the next room, and I felt alone in the universe. Through my mind flashed the glider I would stumble into at one and three and five in the morning in a state between sleep and wakefulness, an anxious place. How many times would Kassandra let loose that squeaky piglet cry of her immature voice box? Could I soothe her back to sleep? John didn't seem to mind if his daughter stopped breathing. It was my job to keep vigil, bolting upright in bed and willing her tiny rib cage to flutter.

Looming over me was the day, two months from now, when I would resume my job at the ad agency. I was fortunate, everyone said so, to finagle a part-time deal, pro-rating my salary, of course. But I could already see those three days per week for what they were: evil. Everything had changed.

Kassandra was asleep. I extricated myself as if on a stealth mission.

John reappeared. *Sshhh*, I motioned.

"Need a hand?" His tone matched my unspoken sentiment: *What the hell could he help with?*

"I'm fine." I hobbled to my feet, spine hunched. My bottom ached.

John's gaze ping-ponged between wife and child. "I still can't believe she came out of you."

"Mmm." I was not at the point where I could marvel metaphysically. I was still reliving my terror in the delivery room when John croaked, "Oh my God!" as Dr. Roth fished the baby out, prompting me to believe I'd borne a centaur.

I had failed miserably at squatting and giving birth. I said *yes* to the epidural and approved a forceps delivery through clenched teeth: "Just. Get. Her. Out." John stayed close to my metal bed in the frigid operating room, both of us paralyzed by the specter of salad tongs crunching our baby's skull. Zero emergency procedures had been reviewed in the holistic birthing class, where I'd visualized a green meadow while slow dancing with my husband.

"Sh-should I be relieved?" I stammered through an oxygen mask to my obstetrician in heels when the baby finally spurted out and was whisked away by nurses.

"You should be thrilled," Dr. Roth said, stitching me up, fingers flying over my perineum. She was smiling assuredly, but ten minutes earlier, she had been barking to a nurse, "Heartbeat's not up fast enough. Internal fetal monitor, stat!"

Her shouts threatened to confirm my worst fear: I had carried Kassandra for nine months only to lose her at the finish line.

Now, in our bedroom, John and I eyed each other with bewilderment. "Come," he said, putting his arm around me. "Let's look at her."

We looked.

"I'm scared she won't be pretty," I blurted.

"She will be. Look at her mother. She has your toes exactly, the third, the way it curves."

It didn't help, what he said. I was scared. The night scared me.

My father-in-law loomed in the doorway, snapping surgical gloves over his fingers. "You ready?"

My breath caught. I would never be ready.

I leaned down and buried my lips in my sleeping baby, inebriated by her fragrance. *From now on, everything will be for you.*

"Yes." I straightened to face him. "Come on in."

I Know Where He Got That Hair!

Elizabeth Anne Hegwood

After my first son was born, everyone talked about his hair. How pretty, how pale. "Hair like yours," they said. I'd never received many comments about my hair. For most of my life, I have streaked it with chemical lighteners, like every other woman I know whose hair is naturally a shade too light to be called brown. Even with serum and a flat-iron, I have commonplace, unremarkable hair. Now that my baby, Jackson, was here, people were delighted about his cheeks, his ears, his back, his eyes, all of which were the shape of my husband's. *Spittin' image,* they still say. *But what a blondie,* they said. *I know where he got that hair!*

They also talked about his size. A big baby, almost eleven pounds. In the last month of pregnancy, well-meaning mothers asked me questions about what I'd been eating. How big were other babies in my family? Was I *sure* I hadn't developed gestational diabetes? When Jackson was three weeks old, an acquaintance of my mother-in-law scooped him up and asked me what size he wore and how often he ate. I stared at her and then took him back, wondering why everyone seemed to have decided that decorum doesn't apply when speaking about other people's babies. Surely she'd be taken aback if those were the first questions I'd asked her about herself.

My disquiet, though, had started even before Jackson was born. From everywhere came those more experienced mothers who lectured me about vegan diets and legal rights to breastfeed in public. They told me television could be a bad influence on an unborn child. If I objected to any of their advice, they said it was my hormones talking. I understood that well-meaning mothers are impervious to ridicule. But I also let them get to me.

I was already on the defensive by the time Jackson was born, and I only became more so as he got older. No one knew anything about my baby! Yes, he was kind of heavy in the crook of your elbow, but then, I said, his bones were so long. I'd seen fat babies before, rolls on the wrists, eyes squinched up. My baby didn't look like that. The skin on his back was translucent and smooth; his soft thighs were proportioned. When I undressed him, I could see the faint hollows of his rib-cage rise and fall with quick, irregular breaths. If I pointed out that I could see the bone of his sternum, people said, "Oh, but he'll be a big guy. He'll fill out." Then they showed me how long his fingers were, his strong catcher's-mitt grip. WWE, joked my husband's friends. NFL. Every time I insisted that my son's size was all height, people said, "Basketball. Or quarterback." Then they jiggled him around, as if to prove his hardiness, as if his bulk were somehow necessary for his future success.

The grandmothers brought clothes, piles of outfits and stacks of bibs that instructed the baby to call them (the grandmothers) if

I (the mean mother) said no. My mother gave Jackson pajamas with images of cars and pickups and gas pumps, and a train-print Ralph Lauren set more expensive than my own sleepwear. She bought T-shirts with soccer balls, baseballs, footballs, basketballs. My mother-in-law, because my husband loves comics, brought Spider-Man blankets and Batman bibs, but I couldn't help but think that angry-eyed grown men didn't belong on baby stuff. *What ever happened to ducks?* I wondered.

Later, my mother gave Jackson clothes with fire trucks and dump trucks and tractors on them. My mother-in-law sent socks, bibs, a monogrammed blanket, and a baseball hat with a matching pinstriped baseball suit, all in our school's colors, complete with embroidered fighting-eagle mascots.

"Who plays baseball?" I asked my husband.

"No one," he said. I kept looking at him until he said, "What?" "All this sports stuff. It's weird."

"What's weird about it?"

"What do you *mean* what's weird about it? It's like they're totally ignoring my taste." I held up the bib with the eagle mascot. "He's growling. Look at that. He's mad." But really I was turning into the angry one, way out of proportion, and even as I protested I didn't understand why I was responding so dramatically. This wasn't me.

Although I knew I was acting strange, I held up two more bibs, one with a smiling Tigger and another with two babies being friends. "These are better. We have an infant," I said. "Not a little yelling person in fight stance. For Christ's sake, he's tall, but he's a *baby*." I pulled a miniature Superman outfit out of the plastic grocery bag I'd shoved it into. "I'm not putting him in this," I said, holding up the cape.

"Okay," said my husband.

"And, actually, that Superman poster on the wall is too scary."

"If you're not comfortable with it—"

"I'm not," I said. "I never thought I'd care about gender-specific clothes," I said, almost embarrassed that I'd even used the phrase, "but I guess I do."

I knew how my husband was probably looking at me—he doesn't often let me get away with being petty and, besides, he remembered how I'd railed about the other hysterical, self-righteous women—so I didn't look back, but I felt him watching me as I folded up all our gifts and pressed them into a drawer. I tucked away the blue clothes and the green clothes, then put the yellow clothes, with their noncommittal ducks, on top.

A couple of weeks later, I was even more distraught, and in my emotional confusion I picked a different fight with my husband, citing all the comic books and movies he had that were not, I said, what a child should see. After making him promise to weed through everything in the office, I went to Target and spent too much money on the sweetest boy clothes I could find, going for script instead of block letters, picking the word *cute* over *champ*. The basket filled up with forest animals, more greens and browns than blues.

Later, when I got home, my husband and I sat on the couch. The baby was propped in my lap, making those strange deep squeaks which I thought were becoming laughs.

"Who's to say he'll even like loud things?" I said. "Why don't they make boy shirts with quiet things on them?"

"Basket weavers," he said. "Or Petri dishes."

"I'm being serious. He might *hate* comics." My throat was tight.

"Which is fine," my husband said, reaching across the space between us. "Hey."

"This is important to me," I said, edging away, though I didn't know why. None of my reasons made sense, not even to me.

He's a quiet baby. That's an understatement. It amazes people, and they attribute his silence to the fact that he's watching everything. And I find that I am suddenly nodding in agreement, wanting to believe that my son is developing a love for looking, which will later become a love of words. Other times I fantasize that he *does* become unlike me: athletic, boisterous, unafraid, easy with himself in a way that I am not. He may love pictures of heroes and villains more than pictures of anything else, or he may prefer cars and trucks, mechanical knowledge, to words.

Still, sometimes I pretend as if I don't know his interests may not match mine, and I find myself acting like the well-meaning mothers with whom I've lost patience. I think about the moments when, despite all the love I have for my parents, I decided there were things I couldn't understand about them, things some part of me felt right to judge. Maybe, knowing what I know about the subjects I love—their unpopularity, their inaccessibility, their strangeness—I am aware that if my son does not, on some level, care about them, there will be a moment when I too become kind of ridiculous to him, a moment he won't have the heart to tell me about, and that I, despite having done it myself, won't be able to see.

Oh, Baby

My son is three months old, and his hair is still a lighter blond than my own. People still ask me if the color will stay, as if I can decide. I don't predict whether it will or won't. I'm too distracted by the other changes, both in him and me. Often it feels as if he and I develop new skills, new preferences, new anxieties because of, rather than in spite of, each other. Most days I feel joyful and nervous, eager for whatever change comes next, thankful that we, as people, change at all. And I finally get it: This blond boy *isn't* mine. He is his own.

But there's always a moment, even in the most magical days, when, overcome with fear, I want to read my child every book he has, then read them again, or take him outside into the chilly, golden air to show him the watermark of a moon, waiting for his eyes to finally lock on it. I kiss his yellow velvet hair, looking for these other moments to postpone the inevitable, the first time we will fail to recognize each other.

Hungry

Amy Amoroso

When my daughter Maeve was born, she couldn't nurse. She lost weight for almost two weeks while my milk dried up.

I have spent nearly four years writing and erasing those words. I have made excuses and pushed the facts away, but I have not forgiven myself. Not yet. There are theories about why Maeve couldn't successfully latch onto my breast—cranial bones shifting in the birth canal, food allergies, underdeveloped oral muscles—but I don't believe them. I have my own theory.

My first child, Maeve's older brother Duncan, was born silent and blue. His shoulders were stuck on my pelvic bones, and the vessels of his neck were compressed in the birth canal before I delivered him. For seven minutes after he was born, three nurses pumped his newborn chest and blew oxygen into his mouth. I couldn't reach him from where I was in the bed, couldn't move because of the pain in my pelvis from pushing him through. It was my husband Seth who took his tiny hand and spoke to him. Then, finally, Duncan took his first breath.

Though Duncan recovered quickly, we never wanted to go through a birth like that again. So the second time around, when I was pregnant with Maeve, there was a plan. Our midwife explained that our risks for another shoulder dystocia were high and that the surest way to prevent it was to schedule a planned caesarean section. This, I knew, also came with risks. I asked if there was anything else we could do. She told me that I should gain as little weight as possible during my pregnancy to keep the baby small, and she would perform a maneuver called a corkscrew in which the baby would be manually turned as she came through the birth canal. It wasn't as preventative as a C-section, but it would lower the risks. *Okay*, I thought. *Let's keep the baby small.*

I didn't realize Maeve was listening.

Of course, it's not exactly accurate to say Maeve heard the midwife and me discussing my weight, because her auditory nerves were only buds at that point. She was no more than four inches long, her heart just beginning to beat, her fingers and toes perhaps still webbed. But surely the sentiment rippled through every cell in my body, including the growing cells that would make up her life. And it came back every time I got on the scale at the midwife's office or at home. It was there when I said no to ice cream, French fries, or cookies. And again when I measured my weight against what it had been in my first pregnancy. The words *keep the baby small* were there even in the moments just after Maeve was born—still a slick, soft lump burrowing into my chest. "A girl?" I said in shock and wonder as they placed her on my chest. And then, as if by reflex: "How much does she weigh?"

It turned out that Maeve was eight pounds—almost exactly the same weight as my son. The midwife performed the corkscrew move, and the delivery was perfect. In those first two weeks of Maeve's life, I was high on the fact that our birth had been seamless, that my labor was short, and that I now had a healthy baby girl. I didn't know she wasn't getting enough milk. When she fed in small bird-like nibbles and then fell asleep or lost interest, I assumed she simply nursed differently from her brother. But there were other signs. My nipples hurt more. They were cracked and bloody. At times it felt like there were shards of glass being sucked from inside of them. Maeve didn't have the mustard-seed poop that healthy newborns are supposed to have. It was green and shredded, like bits of cooked kale. This, I eventually learned, signals that a baby isn't getting enough milk.

At Maeve's first checkup, our pediatrician saw my sore nipples and put Maeve on the scale. She looked worried. Maeve had lost two whole pounds since her birth two weeks before. This is when my pediatrician, who always encouraged breastfeeding, sent me home with a tub of formula. It was the good kind, probiotic, but I still couldn't use it. I'd read about all the benefits of breast milk, and every woman in my family had breastfed her children. I'd heard the stories of mothers who introduced formula to supplement feedings and whose babies had lost interest in nursing altogether. This couldn't happen with my child. The thought of putting synthetic formula in my brand-new baby's belly was all wrong. The pediatrician explained that—formula or otherwise—Maeve needed to be fed every two hours until her weight increased. Driving home, I felt like I'd failed the most important test of motherhood: I couldn't feed my child.

That night I pulled out my breast pump. After trying to pump a bottle for almost an hour and getting not even an ounce, I was devastated. In the days after Duncan was born, my breasts had been full, leaking, aching to nurse. What was happening? I couldn't believe my milk was gone. Seth went to warm up the formula, but something deep within me didn't want him to. We fought about it. We screamed. Maeve screamed. And after it was over, after sobbing from the pain in my breasts and in my heart from hearing my daughter cry of hunger, of longing, I tried to nurse her. *Come on,* I whispered to her, *only you can make more.* I watched her anxiously in the dim light of my bedroom, which was adjacent to our kitchen. I could hear the sounds of Seth doing dishes. I could see the tub of formula on the counter. Maeve sucked for a while and then fell asleep on my bare chest. She'd given up.

Maeve did not wake for hours. She slept and slept, only opening her eyes for short periods while we changed her diaper or tried to feed her. We found out she was sleeping so much because she was conserving calories. She was shutting down. We were told how serious this was. How she needed to be woken and fed every two hours until she began gaining weight. It is excruciating to wake a newborn baby. Seth carried her in one hand, up near his head like a package, not a baby. He flicked on and off the lights and said her name over and over. But she still slept. He brought her into the cold October air outside. She slept. It took sometimes a half an hour or forty-five minutes to wake her. We warmed up the formula. She didn't want it.

Our pediatrician told us to dress her in warm clothes and keep a hat on her head at all times. This way she wouldn't have to waste calories heating her body. Seth remained focused on logistics, getting Maeve fed, making meals for the rest of us, doing dishes, reading and putting our toddler to bed. I was dried up and desperate. I kept wondering why this had happened to us and what I'd done wrong.

We found a lactation consultant who put me on six capsules of fenugreek and six capsules of blessed thistle a day. I was instructed to pump every two to three hours, but only after attempting to nurse and then bottle-feed. It was a constant cycle of failed nursing attempts, bottle feedings, and pumping sessions. Instead of my newborn child waking me in the middle of the night, it was the electronic beeping of my alarm clock. Then sitting in the living room hearing the swishing sound of the medical-grade breast pump I'd rented from the lactation consultant, the one they used in hospitals for the mothers of preemies too small to nurse. Standing at the kitchen sink at two, three, and four in the morning to wash the parts of the pump. After only a few days of formula, our lactation consultant found us some donor breast milk. She left it on our doorstep on Halloween night in plastic bags with dates written in another mother's handwriting. I was so jealous of that mother and her freezer full of milk. Maeve gulped up the donor milk happily. She seemed alert and awake again. We sighed with relief. But pangs of failure spread through my body.

Within a few days, my milk came flooding back, as our lactation consultant had promised. I was ecstatic and stockpiled my own plastic bags with dates and ounces proudly written in my own handwriting in the freezer. I did not think of anything else but feeding Maeve, *breastfeeding* Maeve. We kept the routine going—try breastfeeding, then bottle feed to make sure she got enough, then pump milk for the next bottle. I weighed her every other day. I tracked her weight and the ounces she drank in a notebook. I inspected her poop for green specks. I nursed my sore and broken nipples, suffering fevers, mastitis, and plugged ducts and fearing that my milk would run dry again. When I got a plugged duct, the milk in that breast would dry up and the whole cycle of worrying about Maeve's weight would start again. But I kept going. Sleep-deprived, humiliated, and fiercely determined, I kept going.

My sister took me on a walk one November day about a month after Maeve was born. She wondered if it was time to let go of breastfeeding. I'd given it more than a shot, and to her, I didn't seem well. I *wasn't* well. Overcome by a sense of failure and shame, I wasn't in my right mind. We had failed Maeve, I thought. *I* had failed Maeve. I was embarrassed to go into public places with bottles when I'd seen so many other mothers just breastfeed quietly anywhere. I'd been one of those mothers with my first child. I'd nursed him in dark corners of restaurants, at friends' parties, and in museums. I had judged other women for not breastfeeding their babies, for propping bottles up on shopping carts or in strollers. I had wondered why they wouldn't do something so simple, so natural, so healthy. Now I transferred that judgment onto myself.

I lied to my sister that day. I told her I was fine, we were getting closer, I could keep going. One plugged duct after another, I kept at it for a second month, then a third.

Maeve, though, was doing better. She was gaining weight and slowly creeping up the growth chart. Our efforts were working, but I was exhausted. At the three-month checkup, I told our pediatrician that I was thinking of quitting. The plugged ducts were painful and unpredictable. I hated living with the anxiety of not knowing if Maeve was getting enough milk. Our pediatrician nodded in understanding. She'd had three children of her own and knew the physical demands of a new baby, let alone a new baby who was having trouble nursing. She reassured me that Maeve had had three good months of breast milk, more than many babies ever get. And there were good formulas out there. But all the while she spoke, I could feel the weight in me drop into my gut. I wasn't ready to let myself give up. Not yet.

When the pediatrician began Maeve's exam, she laid her down on the crinkly paper of the table and gently held her little fists. *It's time to grow*, she said, *to get big and tall. We were worried about you getting stuck on the way out like your brother, but you are safe now. It's time to grow.* This is when it hit me, when the words of my pregnancy came back. *Keep the baby small.* I imagined that the words had seeped into my skin, into Maeve's skin. That they lingered in my breasts and in Maeve's small body, disrupting the exchange of milk between mother and child.

After the doctor spoke, Maeve reached her tiny arms above her head and stretched her toes out, eyes bright, lips parting into an open smile. Then she turned her head and pedaled her feet in a baby dance as if she'd heard every word. *It's time to grow, to get big and tall.*

We kept going. The plugged ducts started to recede. The pumping and bottles in the middle of the night became less crucial. Our labor—both mine and Maeve's—began to pay off. Still, the anxiety about my milk supply and plugged ducts came up each time I nursed Maeve. I tried to push it away. I tried not to stare down at her desperately as she sucked. I wanted to connect with her, but I feared that I would distract her with my eyes. Despite all that had happened, Maeve was a beautiful and charming baby. She loved to giggle and lock eyes, coo and tell me baby stories in the middle of a meal. As sweet as it was, her stopping and starting while breastfeeding made me anxious. To avoid distracting her, I fixed my eyes on what was outside the window of my bedroom: the snow lining brown branches, the budding leaves, the buzzing bees. Whatever the season, I let my focus be outside until I was sure she'd had enough milk.

The memory of failure, pain, and humiliation remained. It roamed from my breasts into my gut. I began to have diarrhea the moment I woke every morning and at odd times throughout the day. I eliminated gluten, dairy, yeast, and eggs from my diet to figure out what was causing my digestive trouble, but it became a battle to figure out what I *could* eat.

Somehow I knew my digestion wouldn't clear up until I freed myself of the emotional burden I was carrying. Determined to rid myself of worry and guilt, I went to see an energy therapist. I spilled my guts to her, sobbing in the dim room while she nodded patiently and listened. She performed a session on me that was aimed at shifting my anxiety and shame from our breastfeeding troubles out of my body and into the universe. *The universe knows what to do with this,* she explained. *You don't have to hold it anymore.* When I emerged from her office that afternoon, something had shifted. I'd been looking down for months, staring at my breasts, my baby, my gut. Coming out of the session, I felt suddenly more aware of the world around me— the sky and wind and trees. Feeling my place in the vastness of the universe made me light and free for the first time in months.

I breastfed Maeve for a full year and then thirteen months, fourteen months, fifteen, sixteen. I slowly began to trust my body and my beautiful baby. I began to trust that she knew what she needed and how to get it. We stopped needing the supplementary bottles and the pump. I was never able to breastfeed Maeve in a room with other people or in public as I had with my son, and I never quite let go of the fear I'd gathered in those first few months of her life. But I did try to release it into the universe as the energy therapist had instructed. The window in my bedroom became a constant reminder to let the worry out, not to hold it. And then, one February day, it was over. On our last night of breastfeeding before I left for an out-of-town conference, I sobbed. My heart and belly ached. I was suddenly empty and relieved, yet profoundly full of sorrow.

I hope Maeve will forgive me. I hope she will understand that I did not want her to stay small for any other reason than to survive birth, to come out breathing and crying and alive. I try to remind myself that I did the very best I could. I was acting out of love—perhaps with blinders on—and I take responsibility for what went wrong. As mothers, we sometimes carry these failures in our bodies the same way we carried our children in the womb. Often it's a matter of delivering them out into the world, writing them down, saying them out loud, and letting the trees and the wind and the sky figure out what do to with the rest.

So what would happen if I told myself that, yes, something did go wrong at the beginning of Maeve's life, but a lot of other things went right? It's true that when Maeve was born she couldn't nurse. It's true that she lost weight for almost two weeks, that I refused the formula and let her cry on my chest, hungry, until she went to sleep. But it's also true that today, Maeve is a perfectly beautiful, healthy little four-year-old. She loves her baby dolls and snuggling with me to read books on our couch. She loves playing with her older brother and picking peas from our garden. She loves olives and ice cream and eggs over easy. And sometimes she walks around naked in her cowgirl boots, pushing her toy stroller with a bag on her shoulder, singing like a spring bird—full of hope and joy and hunger for life.

States of Permanence and Impermanence

Suzanne Farrell Smith

Foam isn't a substance so much as a state of being. When pockets of gas are caught in a liquid or solid, you get foam. It can be dense, like yoga mats, Halloween masks, and swimming noodles, or light, like flame retardant or the head of a beer.

Aside from high-school chemistry class, I've never given foam much thought. Not until now, anyway, as I sit on a foam-filled leather seat in a basement medical office, waiting for my infant son to be called. Tufts of yellow foam peek through a crack in the seat next to me. My fingers reach instinctively to tuck it in but I draw them back. I can't remember if there's hand sanitizer in the diaper bag.

Sebastian has been prescribed a custom-fabricated polyethylene foam cranial remodeling orthosis coated with a flexible plastic shell—otherwise known as a helmet. The helmet's shell will be protective and decorative, too, says the brochure. But it's the foam lining that will be molded to fit Sebastian's asymmetrical head, treating the plagiocephaly—flattening—in the back. The foam will lie flush against the part of his skull where growth needs to be curbed but will sit away from the flat part, allowing the skull to grow out and round like other human heads. And it's the foam that will be adjusted, since my son's dome is growing at a speedy one to two centimeters per month. The orthotist will photograph, measure, scan, feel, and gently direct Sebastian's skull where he wants it to go. Like a bonsai tree.

"Mrs. Smith?"

Yuri, the giant, blue-eyed Russian who will cultivate my son's head, looks a little like Sam the Eagle, a little like a Pixar character, and a lot like my Eastern European relatives. Yuri says I can bring the stroller—"We have parking lot!"—and leads me to a small, windowless room outfitted with two chairs, a desk with a computer and printer, and an open, waist-high black case, about the size of a small coffin, that says *STAR Scanner* on the side. I park the stroller just outside the door where, I see, it will actually block much of the hallway.

"It's very warm in here," I say as I remove Sebastian's knitted hat. Winter approaches, and the heater is on. I wonder if Sebastian will be able to wear a hat over the helmet. Should I buy bigger, stretchier hats? Yuri disappears. Moments later, a wall-mounted air conditioner cranks on and blasts Sebastian and me with a chill breeze. Yuri returns and launches into a practiced introduction. As he explains basic concepts—plagiocephaly, orthotic devices, craniofacial features—he weaves in and out of pitch-perfect humming, like he's jazzing up the appointment with a snappy soundtrack. He reminds me of the guy who sits alone at the end of a karaoke bar on Saturday nights, drinking fruit brandy and grabbing the microphone at the first chords of anything Sinatra.

"Do you think we could turn off the air conditioner?" I ask. Yuri stops talking. His unibrow tightens. He's pegging me as a problem parent—requesting something and then not liking the results—before we've even begun.

With the air conditioner off, Yuri asks if I have any questions. Of course I do. *How heavy is a helmet? Will it pinch him? What does a mother do about winter hats?* But I'm sensitive now, and I don't want to break his rhythm. "Not at the moment," I say.

He slips a stocking over Sebastian's head, turning my son into a baby burglar. We need to eliminate the millimeters caused by hair, he says, though he and I both can see Sebastian is bald. Then Yuri circles the stockinged skull with measuring tape. While Sebastian smiles and bobs on his unstable neck, making Yuri bob with him to read the tape, I watch a middle-aged man with a walker make his way around the stroller into the room across the hall. Once seated on the exam table, he pulls up his left pant leg and reveals empty space. He must be here for a prosthesis, a device to replace a missing part. My son is here for an orthosis, a device to correct a deformed part. Since baby heads grow so fast, Sebastian will wear his helmet constantly until it no longer fits. Whatever state of deformation his head is in when the helmet comes off, it will stay that way for the rest of his life, growing larger throughout childhood but remaining the same, like scaled geometric shapes.

As I watch the man, I wrap my arms around Sebastian to keep him stable. I rest my cheek against his capped head and think, suddenly, of Stephanie Decker. She was in the news many months ago, when she lost her left leg and right foot while protecting her two children during an Indiana tornado.

Victims of tornado outbreaks and other disasters list for reporters what has been lost, but, invariably, their litanies of destruction end with affirmation of what's still here—the victims' families, their own bodies, togetherness. It's just stuff, they say about homes damaged beyond repair. It's just a car, or, it's just a leg. It can be replaced. And I invariably marvel not at their courage but at what looks, for all the world, like good cheer.

When I was pregnant, I told my husband I would be okay if our baby had missing limbs or a genetic disorder or blindness, that I would instinctively know how to parent him. I'd already lost a twin during the pregnancy. I had developed an attitude that is perhaps atypical for expectant mothers: I would be fine with whatever was left. But if our baby was missing the capacity for love and empathy, if he was missing a conscience, if he was a sociopath, I would be stuck. Somehow the state of being a sociopath seemed more permanent than the state of having no limbs.

Sebastian smiles a lot and makes eye contact. But he also worries us. While in utero, he lay very low, head tilted as it pressed against my cervix. His sternocleidomastoid muscle grew longer on one side of his neck than on the other, leaving him unable to turn his head in both directions. The condition is called torticollis, or twisted neck. During his first two months—as my husband and I fumbled through parenting a preemie, hospitalization for jaundice, breastfeeding training, and fatigue—Sebastian lay on his back, head rotated to the right and tilted up at a forty-five-degree angle, his trunk in a perpetual crescent-shaped hitch. Resting his head on only one side caused a secondary condition: his soft baby skull flattened

until it looked like a continental shelf falling off into the collar
of his pajamas.

Sebastian's pediatrician suggested we have him evaluated,
a process that revealed he also has hypotonia: low muscle
tone. While torticollis makes it hard for him to turn his
head, floppy muscles make it impossible for him to hold it up.
Gravity is Sebastian's worst enemy. Sitting, we're told, will
be a long time coming. Crawling is also a distant milestone,
since Sebastian's arms are persistently pronated, meaning
he keeps his arms at his sides, wrists facing down in prone
position. When we suspend him over the floor, his arms
remain rigid (I say like a ski jumper, my husband says like
Superman) and, should we let him fall, he would fall on his
face every time. He lacks protective reactions.

Neurologists, physiatrists, physical and occupational therapists, and his pediatrician discuss cerebral palsy and muscular
dystrophy and brain masses and infarcts and heart defects.
They order X-rays, ultrasounds, blood work, an MRI, and
genetic tests. Most reveal nothing: a minimally elevated muscle
enzyme, a tiny dot on his cerebellum, an enlarged space
between his brain and skull. Doctors say time will provide
answers. While we hover in our holding pattern, observing
him carefully for improvement or regression, Sebastian under-
goes seven therapy sessions a week—physical, occupational,
and music—that he seems to think of as play time. Without a
diagnosis, we must wait on more targeted treatment. But the
flatness we can try to remedy now.

While I hold my wobbly son, he shows Yuri a new dis-
covery, his tongue, and starts to hiccup. In the stocking cap,
Sebastian's head now reminds me of a bust used to display

wigs. Yuri tells me that's how helmets are made. A bust is created. Layers of plaster are added to fill out the flat part, creating a better-proportioned version of my son. The foam will be molded to the more perfect bust, so the helmet fits the potential head, the hoped-for head, rather than the head my son has. Twenty-three hours a day, for up to six months or even longer, Sebastian will wear a foam wish.

Without the helmet, it's unlikely Sebastian's head will ever round out, which wouldn't matter except the skull plates have to go somewhere. They are protruding over his left brow and shoving his right ear forward. Long-term, he could develop problems with vision, hearing, swallowing, and sinuses. The flatness is also making it hard for him to turn left and right, to roll. Plus, if he's going to have another condition—something more sinister underlying all this, something life altering or even life shortening—I really want him to have a round head.

Next, Yuri asks me to place Sebastian in the coffin-like scanner and keep him still. He wiggles and kicks until Yuri tells me to hold his feet in place. He turns on a Buzz Lightyear toy above Sebastian's head, which does no good. "Make a noise," I say to Yuri. "Cluck or whistle. He likes bird sounds." Yuri says *bawk bawk*, and Sebastian stares at him wide-eyed. His body stops moving.

The scanner records measurements of Sebastian's head and sends them to the computer. The screen shows a bird's-eye-view diagram of his head shape along with a chart of twenty-four dimensions. Yuri explains that the most important number is the "oblique diagonal difference." The measurement from front right to back left should be about equal to that from front left to back right. On a normal human head, the difference between these two diagonal lines is up to three millimeters. Yuri tells me that a difference from three to six millimeters indicates a mild deformity, six to nine is moderate, over nine is major, and anything over eleven counts as severe. Sebastian's oblique diagonal difference: fifteen millimeters. "Very flat," says Yuri. "Very, very flat."

Now I ask my questions about the helmet. How do we put it on if there are no hinges? (It's foam, so it's flexible; there's one break over the ear, and that's where we pry it open.) Does it take two adults? (Two is better, since Sebastian can't hold up his head.) What if Sebastian can't sleep? (He will. Eventually. They all do.) What about cleaning? Yuri warns me about the smell. "Helmet will smell like foot," he says. Yuri, as it turns out, doesn't use articles, so the helmet has become Helmet. "Rub with rubbing alcohol each night. Once a week, wash out with baby shampoo. But don't submerge, because Helmet is foam."

At the end of the hour-long appointment, just as Sebastian is getting cranky, Yuri says I need to choose the helmet's plastic outer coating. He sticks a laminated sheet on my lap and waits. I glance at the thirty or so choices called "fun patterns": Butterflies. Dolphins. Camo. Under Yuri's gaze, I suddenly feel nervous about making this one-time choice, as if my son's socialization will be affected by how others react to the particular design on his head.

I ignore the white. When I searched online for helmet tales, I saw parents who decorated white helmets, but I've got no graphic artistry on paper, never mind on a curved surface. I eliminate anything else light, on account of dirt. Out goes the yellow, the pink, the melon. I strike the hospital blue: too much like scrubs. Sea-foam green reminds me of cheap motel curtains or throw pillows on a Florida lanai. I eliminate most of the pictures, too. Many are cartoonish. Skulls, too ironic.

While I study my choices, Yuri croons to himself—*doot doot doooo*—which makes me want to finish quickly. Skipping to the darker shades, I find the perfect one right away: night sky. Deep purple blue and dotted with bright stars, some golden, some firefly green. Each evening, between book and lullaby, my husband and I darken the nursery and lie on the floor with our son for what we call "starlight." A turtle toy projects stars on the ceiling, and we talk about big dreams and everything he might see and do someday. Sometimes we just lie together quietly, appreciating the limited time he will be a baby, breathing at three different rates. I don't know yet if my son should wear the helmet during starlight. If we put it on right after the bath, his head might be too damp. If we wait until just before we plunk him in his crib, he might be fussy and have trouble falling asleep. Should he be re-helmeted during starlight? Suddenly, this question, of all my questions, looms largest.

Night sky, I tell Yuri. He hums me through the paperwork. I hand my credit card to the secretary while Yuri singsongs a hello to his next patient.

At home, my husband and I eat dinner while Sebastian sucks from a bottle. By now, I've mastered eating dinner with one hand, since Sebastian has not mastered gripping his own bottle. I hate the leaky bottles we use, but they were handed down to us for free and Sebastian won't need bottles forever. Bottle use, like torticollis, like the helmet, and like foam, is temporary. All of this, this babyhood, as much as we enjoy it, we hope is temporary. We hope our son grows more independent. Sits up, crawls. Develops normally. We hope he will, at some future time, leave us. But only temporarily, only until he comes back to visit.

What's the difference between foam and froth? I ask my husband as I tilt the bottle back into Sebastian's mouth. He looks it up. Froth is even more temporary, he tells me. Skim it off the surface of the sea and as the bubbles pop, it disappears. Foam lasts longer. The denser it is, the longer it lasts. Depending on the substance in a state of foam, it can last forever. The polyethylene in the helmet, derived from petroleum, doesn't biodegrade. I believe we will always have Helmet, find perches for it, on my son's trophy shelf some day, on the banister in our dreamed-of house, on my husband's Emmy statue or a pile of my books. Like baby shoes and handprints, the helmet will conjure this time in this small apartment with this small baby.

Sebastian will have some form of torticollis forever, too. His physical therapist tells us that at fifteen, and even fifty, he may revert to his "position of comfort"—head looking right and tilted up—when he's unwell or tired or worried. I don't think I'll tell him. It'll be a good measure of whether he's actually sick when he asks to skip school.

The helmet is ready in two weeks. The morning of the fitting, like every morning, I kiss my son's head and smell his lavender soap. When we arrive to pick up the orthosis, an elderly woman is sitting in the waiting room, wrapped in a long raincoat and wearing a wool hat and scarf, gloves, and boots. I'm surprised to find myself curious whether she's here for an orthosis or a prosthesis. I'm disappointed that I can't see beneath all her layers.

I hear Yuri before I see him, singing loudly over the buzz-saw sound of the machine that trims, sands, and molds devices to fit patients. "Helmet is ready! Helmet is here!" When he places it on Sebastian's head for the first time, my son doesn't flinch. Yuri spends a half hour explaining how to put it on and take it off, though it's actually quite easy. Despite all the singing, I think Yuri takes his job very seriously. He should, seeing as he gives people feet and outfits kids with braces to fix scoliosis. But I've decided I don't like Yuri very much. I should probably find him delightful, but his gaiety in this shabby medical cellar overpowers me, like too much cologne.

On our first night with the helmet, I scrub the lining with a cotton ball soaked in rubbing alcohol. I'm hoping to ward off the smell before it has a chance to build. The helmet costs nearly three thousand dollars, and we don't yet know if insurance will cover any portion of it. I consider other items in our apartment, like laptops and appliances and even our wedding rings, and conclude that this foam helmet is the single most valuable thing we own. Since it's molded precisely to my son's head, it would be worthless if stolen, unless my son was stolen along with it.

Because of the helmet's shape, Sebastian now looks like a character from the old animated show *Speed Racer*. Because of its style, he looks like a space explorer. During starlight, as he shakes his head left and right, testing the helmet, I decide that for the next few months my son will be Speed Racer Space Agent Sebastian, as if there are other Speed Racer divisions, like desert and marine. He'll be off every evening like this one, during starlight and beyond, to cruise the galaxy and protect the planet from candy-stealing enemies, to do anything he wants to do. In space, in a state of weightlessness, you don't need to hold up your own head.

Apocalypse Now

Amy Penne

> *I worry that my son might not understand what*
> *I've tried to be. And if I were to be killed, Willard,*
> *I would want someone to go to my home and tell*
> *my son everything—everything I did, everything*
> *you saw—because there's nothing that I detest more*
> *than the stench of lies. And if you understand me,*
> *Willard, you will do this for me.*
>
> —Kurtz to Willard, *Apocalypse Now*, 1979

I recently asked my kids about their first memories.

"What was it?" I asked. "What's the first thing you can remember?" Without thinking, both recalled early images of bold blue macaroni and cheese boxes. They had consumed Kraft by the case at daycare.

"You don't remember anything before eating macaroni and cheese?" I pressed. I was fishing for proof my parenting fuck-ups weren't set in stone, floating around in their psyches like a laminated list already prepared for their future therapists.

"Nope," Andrew, my youngest, assured me. "I just remember playing at Amy's house and eating mac and cheese."

Relief set in. Thank God for the hypnotic effect of video games, *Finding Nemo*, and processed cheese products. I hadn't been discovered. They don't know.

I hate babies. I fucking hate 'em. Though I birthed a couple, was one, and acknowledge that everyone I know must have been a baby, I'd rather take my rotund shape out bikini shopping in bright fluorescent lighting with my mother-in-law after eating three helpings of shrimp and broccoli Alfredo than coo over babies, pretend they're cute, or lie to unsuspecting parents that their baby looks any different than every other swaddled and gurgling creature at the hospital. Babies, I've learned, rob us of life, liberty, and the pursuit of happiness; they're anti-constitutional.

I've always hated babies. I didn't even enjoy *being* a baby. My first memory is of standing in my own crib screaming my lungs out at my tired mother. Perhaps this explains why I'm an only child.

I grew up in Georgia, where the only moneymaking options for a gangly preteen girl were babysitting or prostitution. Since the latter was illegal and possibly dangerous, I chose the former to earn the money to buy a second copy of Fleetwood Mac's *Rumours*, having thoroughly worn out and scratched up my first one. I learned early on that babysitting young kids wasn't so bad. After all, they're easily placated with television and macaroni and cheese. Babysitting *actual* babies, on the other hand, plunged one into the eighth circle of hell, which I believe is only one step above being frozen in your own shit.

Babies do one thing: they demand. Whether it's food, wiping, shoulders to puke on, or pacifiers, they pull you into their own shit and demand more. After one particularly harrowing session of babysitting, Baby-in-Crib (whose name I've either forgotten or deliberately purged) screamed at me so loudly that I all I could do was curl up, fetal position, in the corner of its nursery. I pulled myself together enough to feed it and change it and keep it safe for a couple of hours until its owners returned from their date night. I stopped babysitting babies after that. Later, in college, I worked briefly as a nanny. There was a standoff with a six-month-old. I lost. That's all I'm legally obliged to say.

I don't have a good explanation for most of what I've done, including becoming a mother. Some primordial urge must have set in when I was three years into an otherwise blissful marriage. At least I think it was blissful. I've got kids now. I can't remember.

A craving to propagate the species infects some of us at a vulnerable age for reasons that only God and Darwin understand. The copulating part of this whole process is great—over too soon, but great. However, the forty-week gestation period followed by infancy? That first time around, it's boot camp. You've got this outside force compelling you to obey, bending your will, breaking you down. That first tour of duty is the longest.

"The Horror! The Horror!"

William was born in the middle of a hell-hot August to parents with too few skills, living in a steamy, two-bedroom apartment near the University of Illinois. My husband Bryan and I were graduate students, working our way through various degree programs to put off the inevitability of real life. But real life can't be delayed when you're carrying nearly ten pounds of dude inside of you, a dude who eventually attempts an exit just below the left lung. William never turned, never got into position, never did anything but suck his thumb in utero, urinate, and kick the piss out of my bladder. He couldn't even manage to get out on time. Two weeks past his due date, he was content just to sit there, contorting my torso and rewiring my colon to suit his emerging limbs. My OB/GYN was on vacation the week William was due, so I consoled myself that managing to hang on in the sweltering heat was good, since it meant Dr. Shepherd would be back to facilitate the "blessed event."

The details of birth are redundant and repetitive: push, breathe, scream, curse, try not to take the sharp objects away from the medical professionals so you can stab the responsible party.

William didn't cooperate, so they shot me up with Pitocin, the induction cocktail, which I endured for about twenty-two hours. Thankfully, Dr. Shepherd needed to get to a party that night, and when he decided he was bored waiting for me to deliver, the nurses pitched the Pitocin and slapped me down on the table for a speedy C-section. Actually, the chatter between Dr. Shepherd and his nurses about his impending party kept me preternaturally calm in the middle of the chaos that is surgical delivery. Emergency sections are very different beasts from planned ones; my second son, Andrew, with the giant-but-healthy head, arrived via a planned and particularly organized C-section. Those are downright leisurely. I'd do that again any morning: have baby extracted, do some mild nursing by midday, then enjoy a little happy-hour gin and tonic at four. But the last-minute emergency variety left me resentful of William, who necessitated the drugs, the shaving, the strapping down of my arms, and the colon cleanse a nurse performed on me because my bowels had shut down after the trauma. We were not on good terms when he got here, and his incessant screaming upon arrival didn't endear him to us immediately. Yet we managed to get this squirming pile of flesh into the infant car seat and safely back to our suddenly tinier apartment.

As in my early babysitting endeavors, I managed to feed him, change him, and keep him healthy and safe—except this time, no parents were coming back after date night. No one was coming to relieve me. He stayed with us, curdling our nerves from five every afternoon until he passed out just before ten at night. He was inconsolable. *What to Expect When You're Expecting* doesn't inform the reader that the life-sucking malady known as colic will steal your soul and tempt you to make a deal with the devil at the crossroads if only this kid will shut the fuck up. Seriously, editors, get that into the updated fifth edition.

"Saigon. Shit. I'm still only in Saigon."
Gas drops. Baby Tylenol. Rocking. Nursing. Nursing upside down, on the left side. Sleeping with the head in an upright position. Sleeping in the bouncy seat. Putting the baby down. Letting him cry it out. Picking the baby up. Driving around the neighborhood. Sound machines with whooshes of the ocean or a mother's wombed-up heartbeat. Special bottles that limit air in the baby's tummy. Trips to the pediatrician. (They love those, at $250 a visit). Listening to a mother-in-law, who claims everything will be fine, and talking to helpful neighbors, who prescribe shots of whiskey.

We tried them all. Some remedies worked for a tiny bit of time, but escape was the only consistent antidote. I resorted to making multiple trips to the grocery store between five and ten in the evening. I dashed to the store at 5:45 p.m. for diapers and again at 6:15 for gas drops, followed by a final 8:30 trip to get some toilet paper. Anything to avoid the baby. My husband would remember we needed milk and then, two hours later, he'd go back for a box of Cocoa Puffs. Between excursions, we managed. Barely. But only because of the Cocoa Puffs and *The Waltons* reruns, with their infectious family bonding. And boxed wine, left over from our friends' wedding.

Late one hot August night, about two weeks after William was delivered, Bryan and I sat sobbing on the edge of our bed, the very same bed that had conspired with us in this act of procreation, wondering when those proverbial "real parents" would come and get him. We were grateful he was healthy and normal and had all those feelings parents are supposed to feel. But we wept.

"Damn it," I cried, sobbing so hard the bed rocked. "This . . . feels . . . like . . . a war zone."

"I know," was all Bryan could get out through his own broken sobs. Bryan is quiet, introverted. He never complains because that would draw attention and take effort. Agreeing with me that he felt we had made a huge mistake was like Mother Teresa admitting publicly that cleaning the lepers in Calcutta sucked.

We were sure we were inadequate and inept. William was a perfect baby, except for the colic, and he deserved parents who knew what the fuck they were doing. Not us. We were losers.

"Saigon. Shit. I'm still only in Saigon." Martin Sheen's improvised madness at the beginning of *Apocalypse Now* kept replaying in our heads day and night. They—in-laws, midwives, people from Walton's Mountain—tell you that having a baby is the greatest moment in your life, a real turning point. That's true. It is a turning point, but one with innumerable casualties. Bryan and I had to face the fact that we'd been attacked. We'd never been so vulnerable.

"Horror . . . Horror has a face . . . And you must make a friend of horror."
Not only did I get hit from the front with William's colic, I was flanked from the rear by postpartum depression. Postpartum depression is the face of horror.

Like a good scholar-mom, I researched solutions. My favorite helpful advice comes from the Mayo Clinic's website: "Postpartum depression isn't a character flaw or a weakness. Sometimes it's simply a complication of giving birth. If you have postpartum depression, prompt treatment can help you manage your symptoms—and enjoy your baby." Indeed, postpartum depression is a complication of birth. Enjoy your baby? You mean the blood-curdling screams, the engorged breasts that have to be pumped at work, the spit-up perma-stains on every article of your clothing, and the bondage to a colicky creature who keeps you from date night? I'll be sure to remember all of that during my leisurely stay in rehab. Thanks, Mayo.

Friends, you think. You'll call friends. Good idea. Wait, but your friends all *adore* rocking their little ones at two in the morning, quietly singing them back to a gentle sleep after nursing, listening to *Baby Bach,* and finally turning on the plastic fish aquarium that swirls magical realism all over the freshly painted nursery like an acid trip with Hunter S. Thompson. Your friends and family *already* think you're an asshole because you're not finding that the joys of infancy match the charming version of babyhood perpetuated by America's Disney-addicted culture.

As a last resort, I checked with my doctor. After a month of uncontrollable crying, I figured this was beyond the "baby blues" *What to Expect* had described. This was dark. I was in the shit. Dr. Shepherd said it was normal and offered me a mild antidepressant. But again, I did my research, and—like my other new-mom friends—I was nervous about drugs in my breast milk. Even though it's supposedly safe for babies, this particular antidepressant's ever-increasing list of side effects includes sleepiness, nervousness, insomnia, dizziness, nausea, skin rash, headache, diarrhea, upset stomach, loss of appetite, abnormal ejaculation, dry mouth, and weight loss. Great. So I'd be less sad but abnormally ejaculating. No thanks.

"I love the smell of napalm in the morning."
Babyhood invites mothers—the good ones—to spontaneously visit. Friends, your Episcopal priest's wife, and your sweet cousin all seem to find their way to a mother in need. Babies can provoke terror in those of us under the influence of post-partum depression, but they can also inspire pure unadulter- ated kindness in people who have survived the Burroughsian Interzone of infancy and lived to tell about it. That is how we

have survived as a species. Evolution be damned: we've survived because of the tenacity of hearty Episcopalian women.

It was week four of hell. I'd turned down Dr. Shepherd's antidepressants. I was suffering from a horrific rash under my swollen, nursing breasts. I had already gone back to work just three weeks after William was delivered; I had no maternal leave, just a handful of sick days.

I was grading a set of papers on a Saturday in late September when I heard a quiet knock on our apartment door. It was Mary Hallett, the hearty, no-nonsense wife of Father Tim Hallett, pastor at St. John's Episcopal Church on campus, where Bryan and I had been wed three years earlier. I expected the pastor's wife to come calling. A few of the kindhearted church ladies had already delivered pans of lasagna and chicken casseroles, and I guessed (correctly) that Mary was here with her signature chicken-noodle soup, a particularly tasty version of the classic healing brew. She handed me the pot of soup and some fresh bread, nodded toward William in his bouncy seat, then turned to me and offered, "Let me grab your laundry while I'm here and I'll take it home for a wash and fold."

It struck me that, unlike all the other visitors, Mary wasn't here to coo at the baby; she was here for me.

"Lord no," I replied, blearily. "That's okay, Mary. I got it. Bry and I are fine."

She looked at me with her gray eyes, brushed her salt-and-pepper bangs to one side, and stated in her efficient Episcopalian voice, "No one is fine after they've had a baby." She pulled out a big mesh bag she'd brought over.

I could see she was serious. I scurried and grabbed Bry's jeans and my bra from the bathroom floor, underwear from a cardboard box in the closet currently serving as a laundry basket, and random shirts thrown off near the bed by two dazed parents flopping down at night in defeated exhaustion. I put everything in the mesh bag and sheepishly gave it all to this woman, my pastor's wife, a woman I knew well but not well enough, I thought, to hand her our undies.

When Mary returned the next day with our fragrant, sorted, and neatly folded laundry, I nearly sobbed. It wasn't anything like the war-zone feeling Bryan and I had a few weeks earlier in our bedroom. Mary handed over the mesh bag of laundry and hugged me. I was overwhelmed by her kindness, unable to even utter a "thank you." I think she could tell I didn't want to let go of her. But I did let go, my eyes welling with gratitude.

"I'll be back next Saturday," she said. And sure enough, there she was with her determined smile and her laundry bag.

I have never forgotten Mary's matter-of-fact benevolence. I felt saved by soup and fresh laundry. Fortified with this reminder that the human heart heals, and nurtured by something as simple as the fresh scent of Tide mixed with a hint of lavender Snuggle, Bryan and I managed to get through those first months without binge drinking, overdosing on antidepressants, or running away to a cabin in Maine. We managed. I hadn't conquered parenting, but I at least felt like this episode had ended with the kind of neighborly kindness so ubiquitous on Walton's Mountain.

Parents get their lives back only if they stop at one baby. Few do. Most of us are possessed by a demon that attacks when your kid is about two or three, infecting your soul and whispering: *Your life can be like* The Waltons. *Every week a new adventure in which John Boy, accompanied by apprehensive younger brother Ben, pulls Elizabeth out of yet another creek while Mama makes her a new dress out of love, grandma's old quilt scraps, and used kitchen towels. Have more kids. Have even more kids. It'll be just like* The Waltons.

The Dark Lord loves seventies television in syndication; it's one of his favorite weapons of mass destruction. I couldn't fight off the demon possession that talked us into a second one. He may have had colic too, I can't remember. The second time around, I said to hell with the side effects and took the damn drugs. I was much happier.

Incredibly, there are moms who thrive on infancy, who continue making babies and manage to can ten quarts of pickles and tomatoes in the process. The Spillmans down the street made seven babies, and each one was a natural-born caretaker for the next brother or sister in line. The Spillmans do great babies; we don't. Bryan and I stopped at two. (Actually, *The Waltons'* demon encouraged me to go for more, but my body couldn't, or wouldn't, sustain another.)

But here's the thing: Babies evolve into smart-ass kids who talk, memorize the track listing to *Led Zeppelin IV* by age three, learn piano, collect football cards, make heart models in sixth grade, and finally learn how not to trump their partners in euchre. Both of mine, now fourteen and eleven, weathered both infancy and toddlerhood and are nicely settled into the hormonal cauldron of high school and middle school, which is, compared to the flashback-inducing horror of babyhood, a cakewalk. (For me, at least, if not for them.)

Toward the beginning of *Apocalypse Now*, Willard hears on tape Kurtz narrating his symbolic nightmare/dream of a snail "crawling, slithering, along the edge of a straight razor . . . and surviving." I've lived on that straight edge, and let me tell you, it's scary but bearable—if only you can laugh and let a nice Episcopalian lady do your laundry.

Just Colic

Leah Laben

He screamed.

First thing every morning, lurching from uneasy sleep to greet a world he seemed to view with mistrust, he screamed. Getting his diaper changed, he screamed. In the car seat, he screamed. Taking a bath, he screamed. Even while nursing, sometimes, he screamed, though it sounded more like drowning. And most every evening, from about 4:30 p.m. until he passed out somewhere between ten and midnight, he screamed unrelentingly.

At two months old, his skin was still yellowed by breast-milk jaundice, but his screams turned his face so red you would never know it. His tiny fists drove his fingernails into his tiny palms. His legs kicked in an uncoordinated rhythm; his back arched. Toothless mouth stretched wide in apparent agony, eyes clenched shut, hot tears streaming down his cheeks, he screamed.

This was not the baby I knew. Like most newborns, he had spent the first few weeks of his life in a drowsy haze. He slept so soundly that my husband, Jared, and I needed to tickle him awake several times a night to make sure he was eating enough. Sure, he occasionally fussed, but mostly he slept. Through long, lazy autumn days I cuddled with him on the couch, watching reruns of my favorite shows and snacking to keep my milk production up. "He hardly ever cries," I told my sister with pride, as if I had something to do with it.

Then, one day, shortly after he turned one month old, Jared and I took him on a short car trip through the foliage-painted hills to meet his great-grandmother. As we chatted with family members in her living room, he began to cry. I arranged him under a blanket to nurse, but to my bemusement, his crying continued. I stood up and carried him back and forth across the room, bouncing and swaying, but he only became more agitated. He cried for the rest of the brief visit, and by the time we left I felt uneasy, as though I had committed some sort of faux pas by being unable to calm my child in someone else's house. He fell asleep on the ride back home, and Jared and I decided that his stomach must have been upset, perhaps from gulping air while feeding from the bottle we had given him earlier in the day.

For the next few weeks, as the crying worsened and lengthened, I continued to find reasons. Excuses, I would come to recognize later. He was overtired. Overstimulated. Too hot, or perhaps too cold. I hadn't changed his diaper quickly enough. I had eaten garlic with dinner. It was surely something passing that I, in my new-parent ignorance, had overlooked, but that I could eventually pinpoint and rectify. I would figure it out and return him to the *good* baby he was meant to be. Throughout my life, I had found success at nearly everything I put my mind to, and having a baby would be no different. I wouldn't be the mother whose baby disrupted playgroup or dinner. No one would roll their eyes or feel sorry for me or opine on what I was doing wrong in raising this child. Tomorrow, I would get it right, and he wouldn't scream.

He screamed.

There is a commonly accepted definition of colic known as the "rule of three." As the American Academy of Family Physicians describes it, when no underlying medical problem can be diagnosed and a baby cries inconsolably for three or more hours per day, three or more days per week, for three or more weeks, she is considered to have colic. My baby could have met the rule of eight, had there been eight days in a week. My life became utterly defined by his screaming, each day a fruitless struggle to soothe him, each evening plunging again into the madness of enduring his howls. I began to mentally classify each day as "good" or "bad." On a good day, he took a long nap or went to bed early, giving us an extra hour or so of calm. A bad day was ceaseless screaming. My mother-in-law, visiting around this time, told my son, "You don't have to cry just because you're awake, you know." But it seemed that, in fact, he did.

Everyone who has ever taken a long flight stuck next to a restless infant knows the discomfort caused by listening to a baby wail. It's impossible to ignore and agitates something deep within our psyches. The noise is so grating, the *New Yorker* reported, that the US military used recordings of a crying baby as a means of psychological torture on detainees at Guantánamo Bay. As every parent knows, when the baby in question is your own, the response is magnified ten times over. It's an itch under your skin that demands to be scratched, a fire that must be put out. When it goes on hour after hour, day after day, week after week, it starts to feel like something eating your brain from the inside out.

He screamed.

Colic has no well-understood cause or effective cure. According to the journal of the American Academy of Pediatrics, organic disease accounts for less than 5 percent of infants presenting with colic symptoms. Instead, most cases of colic are best understood as variations of normal emotional development arising from a diminished capacity to regulate crying duration. But nothing could stop Jared and me, in the deepest days of the colic, from trying every quick fix culled from the farthest reaches of the Internet and piles of parenting books. There were your standards: nursing, cuddling, walking, dancing, car rides, swinging, and pacifiers. Then the slightly more advanced: babywearing, swaddling, whispering, massage, music, hot-water bottles, dark rooms, skin-to-skin contact, and white noise. And finally the specialty items, really so much snake oil: gripe water, gas drops, homeopathic colic tablets, herbal baths, Baltic amber jewelry, and probiotic powders, along with a thousand other worthless tricks and gimmicks. I altered my diet repeatedly, cutting out possible allergens like dairy, onions, and citrus and keeping crying logs in an attempt to correlate his moods with what I had eaten. But the best we could ever do was distract him by moving from tactic to tactic so that we would get a few minutes of relief before he would start again. For a few weeks, bouncing on an exercise ball while wearing the baby in a wrap carrier would quiet his cries and lull him to sleep perhaps one out of five or six times. We clung to this dubious success so fanatically that we took the exercise ball with us, cramming it into the front seat of our car, to visit my parents for a short Thanksgiving dinner. When our cat clawed the ball and deflated it, one day, we spent an obscene amount of money to have a replacement sent overnight. We didn't blink an eye at the cost.

To make matters worse, he was one of those babies who could not stand to be out of physical contact, even for a moment. In the depths of the colic, the moment he was set down—even if he had been soundly asleep in our arms—he would startle awake and become utterly frantic, crying with awful, gasping screams as though in fear for his life. Even if we picked him up right away, he was impossible to soothe and sometimes screamed until he started gagging. There was a stretch of about five weeks during which he was put down literally only for diaper changes. He slept on me, fed on me, and the rest of the time was held either by me or by Jared. Worse yet, he seemed to be angered by sitting in one place. Most evenings, we spent hours walking him around and around, as though we could outrun the howling. We wore a squeaky spot into the wooden floor of our living room, carrying him in circles night after night. We tuned the television to *Jeopardy!* and *Wheel of Fortune*, as if it were a normal evening in a normal household, but we couldn't even hear the shows over his crying. We had to yell if we wanted to say something to one another, and after a while we mostly didn't bother. By the time, late into the night, that the baby finally passed out and we could take him to bed, I would be shivering with distress.

He screamed.

I rarely left the house or talked to anyone on the phone, because the baby was sure to launch into a fit if I tried. There were days when I didn't want to get out of bed and face what was coming. It was like a physical weight on my chest, the impending hours upon hours of doing my best to help him and having nothing work. Each day was exhausting, and I could see no end in sight. I seldom showered, feeling guilty about leaving Jared alone with him for the twenty minutes it would have taken to wash myself. I didn't change out of my pajamas, and when I managed to eat, I ate with one hand while holding him with the other. There were times when I gave up and just sat on the couch. I let him cry on me, unable to stand up and launch into the useless soothing routine again. His screaming sent my mind into a strange state where things appeared both fuzzy and sharp at once, my eyes rapidly shifting focus, as if my brain couldn't process any information beyond *the baby is crying.* Through the windows I watched the dwindling fall sunlight slanting through beautiful red and gold leaves, set to a soundtrack of torture.

I began to have strange and illogical thoughts about the origins of his colic. I had worked at a high-stress job while pregnant; maybe my anxiety had been infused into his personality in utero. I had reportedly been a colicky baby myself; maybe this was my comeuppance for the crying to which I had subjected my parents. Jared and I had undergone fertility treatments to conceive; maybe the baby was angry because he hadn't wanted to be born at all. There were times when it was so hard not to resent him as he was squirming in my arms, wailing in my face for the sixth hour in a row, and I would think, *Why did I go through all those hormone injections and ovarian ultrasounds just to have my life ruined like this?* And then guilt would wash over me. *Maybe he's like this because he knows we don't love him enough.*

He screamed.

Jared and I had been together for seven years before the baby, and we had always enjoyed an easy, companionable, and loving partnership. We knew that a baby would change our romantic relationship, even strain it. But in the onslaught of our baby's tears, we lost all sense of humor and perspective. I grew convinced that Jared sought out tasks like going to the grocery store, replacing the kitchen faucet, or clipping grapevines in the yard to avoid holding the baby. His trips to the bathroom took longer than plausible, and I knew that he was just hanging out in there with his laptop, shirking. I spent most days in the grip of resentment, silently exhorting him to take the goddamn baby already and let me have some peace. When he finally did so but failed to calm the crying, I would snatch the baby back, suddenly desperate to martyr myself and prove my maternal love. Despite this, I never considered that my marriage might be in danger, that we might be playing out the beginning of the end with every evening we went to bed with no goodnight kiss. I thought of Jared only in terms of his usefulness—or lack thereof—in getting the baby to stop crying.

One evening, we attempted an elaborate soothing maneuver recommended in a book written by a well-known parenting expert. Under a warmed blanket, Jared would hold the naked baby against his bare chest. The rhythm of Jared's breathing, the sound of his heartbeat, and the feel of his breath against the baby's head were supposed to lull the baby right to sleep. But by the time we had warmed a blanket in the dryer, stripped the baby of his clothes and diaper, and set the two of them up on the couch together, the baby was near delirious with screaming and didn't even seem to register the cuddling attempt. I had been envisioning sitting in blessed solitude for a few minutes while the two of them dozed together. Instead I took the baby back, his slight ten pounds like the weight of all that was wrong with the world, and glared daggers at Jared for his inadequacy. I'm sure I must have seemed like an awful stranger to him, crazed, hormonal, and nasty. We moved around each other in cold silence, anger growing with no outlet as the weeks dragged on, snow began to fall, and the colic continued.

He screamed.

I breathed not a word of this to any of my friends or family. I assured everyone that we were happy. Over the moon, of course. The words sounded stupid and hollow, an obvious lie, to my own ears even as I said them. But how could I admit the truth? This was just colic. People had babies all the time, every day. People had babies in horrible poverty, abusive relationships, or no relationships at all. People had babies with heartbreaking defects and diseases. People had two or more babies at a time. How could I tell someone that my one healthy baby was driving me insane, that my productive, committed husband was filling me with rage? It never even occurred to me to ask for help. That would be tantamount to admitting failure at the most important task I had ever taken on. I was consumed with the growing conviction that I was a bad mother, but this was a secret to be kept between my baby and me, not to be shared with the world.

He screamed.

He screamed.

He screamed.

The winter holidays approached and we joylessly decorated a tree and wrapped presents. The day before Christmas,

I awoke, as usual, to my baby thrashing and flailing, letting out a shriek that felt like sandpaper on my face. I offered him a pacifier, which he refused, instead ratcheting up the volume of his wails. A horrible, desperate anger welled up inside me and I flung the pacifier across the room, where it landed in cobwebs that hadn't been cleaned since before he was born. Gritting my teeth, I scooped him up and carried him to the changing table, not bothering to warm my cold hands before I touched his naked skin. He screamed and twisted as I cleaned him and got him dressed. Then I laid him down on the nursery rug, laid myself down beside him, and began to cry too. As I cried, I kept telling him, as if this were somehow the worst part of the whole ordeal, "Christmas is supposed to be fun." We cried together until he fell asleep again, and I just lay there, staring out the window at the sky, watching the bare tree limbs rattling in the winter wind.

And then he stopped.

Had I been someone with religious leanings, I might have attributed the sudden silence to a Christmas miracle. But in truth, as the American Pregnancy Association reports, as a baby reaches three months of age, colic disappears on its own in about half of all cases. And Christmas Day happened to be my baby's three-month birthday. Just like that, it was over. I felt like the survivor of a shipwreck, flung to shore.

Two months. Two measly months was all it had taken to introduce me to the worst parts of my own nature, to turn me into someone who could get angry at her own child for things he couldn't control, who would rather snarl at her husband than comfort him through a time of stress. Through the following weeks and months, my baby continued to be fussy, needy, and clingy, quick to rile and slow to calm. But the eardrum-shattering, brain-melting colic fits were gone for good, and in their absence we began to build our new life on the shores of the strange land known as parenthood.

It would take six more months for us to repair the damage to our marriage. It was hard for either of us to believe or acknowledge how easily we had been blown apart. I don't remember which of us had the courage to first turn to the other and acknowledge that our relationship was in dire straits. I suspect that it was Jared; left to my own devices, I imagine I would have remained locked in my own miserable anger for far longer, perhaps too long to have ever broken free. After the floodgates were opened, however, we discussed it endlessly, desperate to understand why, in the first real test of our marriage's strength, we had failed so utterly. It would have been easy to blame the baby and his insatiable needs. But the truth was that, for as long as we had tried to conceive a baby, neither of us was prepared to accommodate the particular baby we wound up with. Having a baby is essentially inviting another person permanently into your family—a person whom you have never met before. The reality of having the new family member arrive and appear to hate our guts was something for which we were in no way prepared. It required a huge mental adjustment, and we took out our confusion and distress on each other.

None of the baby preparation classes we had taken or the parenting books we had read had warned of the potential damage to our marriage when the infant arrived on the scene. In one class, we had practiced breathing while holding ice cubes in our hands for thirty seconds, time perhaps better spent rehearsing the words *please help me.* To be fair, our experience is not the norm for new parents. Nevertheless, a gentle reminder that our partners are human, just as vulnerable to burnout and disorientation as we are, would have been immensely helpful to us and, I suspect, to most first-time mothers and fathers. Through many hours of earnest conversation, Jared and I found our way back to that truth, back to the compassion and love we had always felt for one another. We pledged that, moving forward, we would base our relationship on deliberate communication and generosity. We take care to remember that we are each a crucial support system for the other and that we are far better for it, both as a couple and as parents.

Today, our son is a talkative, energetic, and mostly delightful four-year-old. I do not take credit for his positive traits, nor do I accept blame for his shortcomings. He taught me the folly of believing that your baby is an extension of yourself. He came into the world proclaiming his personhood in a way that could not be ignored. Had he been a happy baby, an easy baby, a *good* baby (a term I now despise), I would likely have sailed through his infancy patting myself on the back for my own deft parenting choices, rather than thanking my lucky stars and genetics. But I no longer believe all the books and authorities with their One True Method of Parenting that will yield up the child of your dreams. The child of your dreams is just that. The child that you actually get is likely to be as complicated, messy, and frustrating as any other human being on the planet. It may be that nothing you try, nothing at all, can change him. That is what I wish I had understood during those long hours of searching for a nonexistent cure for my baby. He didn't need me to fix him; he just needed me to wait it out with him. He wasn't screaming, "You're a bad mother." He was just screaming. Because it was just colic.

Baby Card

Terrance Flynn

"Please. You gotta see this."

The panic in my voice startles me, but the nurse keeps working. I am a piece of her work. She claimed me as such an hour ago when she checked my wristband and declared, "Okay. You are my transplant."

My iPhone is pointed at her as she moves around my hospital bed. She glances at the baby picture of my six-month-old girl—huge eyes, cartoon-red cheeks, stark-raving bald. My favorite photo. The nurse tightens her lips into a polite smile, but her eyes are so uninvolved I know she hasn't seen it.

She is right to resist. People will dump their lives on you if you let them, all the while acting as if they are doing you a favor. It's called sharing, and I'm not beyond it. The weight of my phone is a brick at the end of my extended arm; still, I hold it out to the nurse. I need her to really see my daughter. A drop of sweat rolls from under my arm, down my torso, and tickles my ribcage like the creeping of a fly.

Over her shoulder: "We need to have you ready in twenty minutes."

The heart-transplant process starts randomly enough, with an unfortunate accident that kills someone's brain but spares the heart. Everything from that point on is careful and constant coordination. All the parts are moving, even the stopped ones like the disembodied heart—frozen and drugged into paralysis, then rushed to where it can be of use. It is best transplanted less than two hours after removal, the duration of my daughter's afternoon nap. Cells begin to die after this amount of time; decomposition happens by the second, even as the heart is being packed in sterile ice. So in the preoperatory stage, there's not a lot of time for the sharing and liking of images.

Even so, I tell the nurse, "You really gotta see this."

She unhooks one of my plastic IV bags, nearly sucked dry and collapsing into itself, prunelike. Plasma is being added to quickly thicken my blood for surgery; it needs to hit a sweet spot of viscosity, somewhere between water and honey. At family dinners, my mother used to thicken her gravy by stirring in cornstarch. She then poured it from a porcelain dish she called a gravy boat. My dad used the phrase *gravy train* as a way of calling people lazy if they rode it. My mom and dad are speeding in her car, trying to get here before I'm wheeled down the hall. They are too old to be rushing like that to an event like this.

The standoff continues with the nurse. My arm aches. My phone goes dark, so I refresh it. The nurse continues working in an ellipse around me, just out of my reach, as if I will grab her if she gets too close.

My partner James has been gone for five minutes. Ostensibly, he's down the hall in the restroom, but we both know he is taking a break. I envy his ability to walk away from my body. Nothing more needs to be said between us; *goodbye* carries too much heft. *I love you* is very one hour ago. By the time we dropped our baby at my sister's and hustled to this room, James and I were exhausted from risk calculation, a little tired of each other.

His absence allows me to panic more productively. Nothing wastes an adrenaline high more than the presence of loved ones. They dissuade you from dwelling on the unthinkable. But very sick people need to take inventory. Item one: my fear of the strange technicians who will change my heart. I am no one to them. A patient, yes, but not a someone. Item two: More than my own death, I fear the estrangement from my daughter that would necessarily follow. What would a six-month-old brain do with my absence? A brain that age is streamlined for the future; it has no aerodynamic drag of nostalgia or clingy memories. After even five days, a six-month-old doesn't remember a face or the sound of a once-familiar voice or the smell of someone's neck.

"Please," I say to the nurse. This time she comes over and takes my phone. Our fingertips brush. She holds it gently in her palm, smiling and rapt. The skin around her eyes softens, making her younger and older at the same time. It's an intimate thing, watching someone cradle your baby daughter, even digitally.

"Tell Dr. Maggio I am a father."

It feels like an oversight, to say the least, that I have not even met the man who will change my heart. By the time he enters the operating room, I will be deeply anesthetized, unable to introduce or speak for myself. So I ask her again: "Will you please tell him I have a six-month-old girl?" She smiles at me as if I am asking rhetorically, but I'm not. Who am I to leave this stone unturned, minutes before heading into a heart transplant? What, am I not going to play the baby card? I need the nurse to inform the surgical team of my fatherhood. Ideally, I'd like her to scrawl at the top of my chart, or with a permanent marker across the skin of my chest, as yet intact: *Family Man! Proceed with Caution.* When I was a gay teen and thought I'd never have kids of my own, I choked on the assumption that parenting makes a life carry more weight and meaning. Worse is the corollary: not having kids makes a life more dispensable. Notice what a desperate hostage says when he has a gun to his head: *Please, don't. I have kids!*

"Tell the surgeon I'm a dad."

The nurse's smile fades, but she touches my arm gently before she returns to work. Not much of a contract, but it will have to do.

James appears at the door, laughing at someone I can't see. When was the last time he and I laughed? I want to apologize for my submerged sense of humor and the unhealthy way I see things now that my heart is lame. Like the other day in the grocery store, when a woman with big teeth stopped me in the frozen foods. She hunched over my cart as if my daughter, bundled in her portable seat, was a collection of meatballs (which she is) and actually said, "Oh, I just want to *eat* her!" All I could do was shiver and say, "Me, too."

I am not myself. Sick people see things differently. To the oxygen-deprived, a gust of fresh air is unsettling, a patch of sunshine too strong against skin made sensitive by medication. Vitality is harsh, offensive even. Medication spiked my nausea for all things sensual. Parenting, for example, became a series of weights, textures, and exuberant pressures. The fierce kick of my daughter's Michelin Man legs, the tug of her hot fist around my bony finger. The voracious way she worked a bottle was as adorable to behold as the smell of formula was repellant. And as she dropped off to sleep on my shoulder, how my eyes watered with the effort of trying to stifle my cough. How I longed for someone to relieve me of her weight.

The nurse leaves in a hurry after saying something to James. He comes to my bed and the vibrancy of my panic fades. We've had the kind of year where my smile alarms him.

"What's wrong?" he asks.

"Nothing." I hide things from him by default, usually too tired to address the catalogue of his anxiety, so we hold hands in silence.

I have nearly died from heart failure several times and in dramatic ways, sometimes in his presence, but my death is not James's worst fear, not by a long shot. The afterlife is what scares him most; that is, his life after my death, specifically the nightmare of his ensuing single fatherhood. To him my death is not the more romantic *without you, I'm nothing*, but rather *without you, I'm a single parent*. To be honest, I also fear his single parenthood, for both his sake and our daughter's. Nothing against him, but who will play sports with her and teach her to sing on pitch? This is my department, while James handles braiding her hair and trips to Michaels craft store, a place to which I am practically allergic. He and I agree that, working together at full speed, we equal one competent parent.

He takes the phone from my hand. I think he is going to turn it off, like before a flight, but he points it back at me. "Talk to her," he says, and I see he is filming.

Coughs are so useful for diffusing emotion. I let loose. When my breathing becomes more regular, I take a sip of water. How can I tell a daughter how to live her best life? Into a phone? The only words that come to mind are *please don't forget me.* "James. Not now," I say, waving my hand at the phone. I'm suddenly conscious of my body in the hospital gown, my matted hair and dry lips, my neck made black and blue from the repeated catheterizations. In the mad dash to get here before the coordinators went on to the next person on The List, I haven't showered. I don't want her to forget me, but I don't want her to remember me like this either.

I have thought about missing out on her life. Mostly late at night, when my hands are so cold I put them against my bare chest and feel only the lukewarmness of a battle being lost. This is when I am curious to know if she will ask about me, and in what terms of endearment or estrangement. My former daddy? Ex-daddy? My other dad who passed away? None of this has been worked out. Another oversight.

James is still pointing the phone at me. A resentment stirs—he will have our daughter all to himself. To raise. To give away.

"Hi, Flynn!" I am straining. "I need direction," I say to James. "Some kind of context, like will you show this to her before prom night? Or her wedding maybe?"

He shrugs.

Not that I think my daughter has to go to prom or get married. James and I aren't even married. We've never been in the right state at the right time, health-wise or geographically.

"Are you still filming?" I ask.

James nods.

"Okay. Honey. I miss you. Be good for Dad." I lick my lips. "Until I come home, I mean." I tell him to turn it off.

He lowers the phone.

"You didn't say 'I love you.'" James shatters his own record for picking the wrong time to critique me. It doesn't help that he is so often right.

"Okay," I say. "Let's do another take."

He holds the phone up again.

"Wait!" I snap. "Tell me when, dammit." My hand goes through my hair, but it's no use. I'm winded from the gesture.

"We're rolling," he says. "I'll just edit the swearing out later."

"I love you, Flynn," I say, and I sound annoyed because I am.

And like that, it's time to go. My mother and father have not made it in time. I text them I love them, then hand my phone to James while I am being wheeled down the hallway on the stretcher. He is told he can go no further, so he kisses my forehead. We unclasp hands, and he stands there helplessly in the cold hall, his arms dangling at his side. I never told him how I much I love his hands.

My desire to live rises in me like nausea, clarifying my own worst fear, which is not my own death. Nor is it that James will fail our daughter. Rather, it's knowing he will succeed, like he does at everything he worries about doing well. Struggle fosters his talents. He will raise our daughter with a skill that my absence will conjure in him.

You think this would be reassuring, but for me, it's harrowing. At some point, probably sooner than later, James will date and find a partner. *They* will probably make the time to get married in some tasteful ceremony.

Cocksuckers.

The night will be so well-planned, it will look improvised. Our daughter will be the flower girl and, my God, why am I so suddenly obsessed with weddings? I've only ever wanted the *right* to marry, not the hassle of actually going through with it.

Maybe when you're facing death, memories hurt less than the absence of them, the dry brittle spaces into which life's so-called milestones might have been rolled but which, for whatever reason, are in the end left vacant.

And the real kicker? The nurses have changed shifts. I played the baby card too soon. I open my mouth to inform the new nurse of my fatherhood, but she covers my face with an oxygen mask, tells me to count backward from ten.

"One, two, three . . ." It's a small rebellion but seems important. She reaches across my body to adjust the flow of something, and I think of my mother's arm stretching across the table to tip her porcelain gravy boat into the depression of my mashed potatoes.

"Four, five, six." My smile comes as a surprise, as does the quirky knowledge that backward and forward are too similar. Married or not, kids or not—the height of irrelevance. I'm going to a place, whatever happens, where even my own heart won't follow, and there is an unexpected freedom. Warmth spreads through me. My vagus nerve will soon be severed, so the words between my brain and my heart are their last. It's a lullaby about a summer day in Michigan. I'm standing waist-deep in the lake behind our house. I've tossed my daughter in the air, and she is blocking the harsh sun just so, creating the perfect shadow on my cooling face. But for the life of me, I can't tell if she will fall back into my arms, or if I'm to watch her float away into an unknowable sky.

The Eleven-Minute Crib Nap

Jill Christman

> *Most of the literature of infant care and psychology*
> *has assumed that the process toward individuation is*
> *essentially the child's drama, played out against and*
> *with a parent or parents who are, for better or worse,*
> *givens. Nothing could have prepared me for the real-*
> *ization that I was a mother, one of those givens, when*
> *I knew I was still in a state of uncreation myself.*
> —Adrienne Rich, *Of Woman Born*, 1976

Babies don't cut deals, and right now my tapping keyboard sounds like the clicking heels of an efficient secretary leading the negotiators into the boardroom. The last thing I want to do is engage. I'd take my laptop into another room, farther away from the crib, but there are too many risks: the scraping of my chair, that squeaky board at the edge of the dining room, the real possibility that a tangle of cords could crash the mouse to the floor. Better I stay put.

I just spent the first hour of what should have been a two-hour nap for Ella nursing her to sleep. She slept, yes, forehead damp with the pleasure of milk and Mama, both of us smelling of honey and salt, her bare toes leveraging my open palm, flexing and pushing and suckling. I can't blame her for wanting to stay in my arms, but I'm a teacher with a pile of grading and a roomful of anxious twenty-year-olds waiting for me in the morning. Everybody wants a piece of me. So with my finger at the corner of Ella's lip, I broke the seal between our bodies. There was a tiny pop as I coaxed my nipple from her mouth. I held a gentle pressure on her chin while her jaw's pumping wound down. Good.

But when I rose from the chair, walked the three steps to the crib with all the stealth of a cat burglar, and started to tip Ella's meticulously supported head toward the mattress, her lids popped open like the long-lashed baby dolls of my childhood with their disturbingly glossy marble-blue eyes. Except in reverse. The eye-popping happened when I lay Ella down, not when I tilted her up. Tip. Pop. Hair-curling scream.

I tried to explain to my nearly toddling daughter that she had this all wrong. I tried to make her understand that our arrangement was only fair. *After all,* I said, wincing and patting her belly in what I intended to be the soothing strokes of all the baby-care books, *I already held you for half the nap! Most babies your age don't have that kind of luck, you know. Some babies go to group care where somebody else takes care of them all day while their mommies work. Can you imagine? But not you. No, sweetie pie. Not you. You get to have half your nap with Mommy, and then you get to have the second half in your crib so Mommy can grade some essays. Mommy needs her hands to grade essays.*

My tone was distinctly Faye Dunaway's in *Mommy Dearest,* and the patting was provoking—too fast, too desperate, not at all pacifying. In that first run at the crib, I'd succeeded not only in waking Ella, but riling her into an uncommon rage. She thrashed, face twisted in fury like the Heat Miser in the holiday cartoon, sweaty hair poking everywhere, her own personal crown of thorns. Ella didn't want to reason with me, and she didn't want to talk compromise.

I scooped her up to begin again. Back to the rocker we went. If suckling at a mother's breast can be disgruntled, that's how Ella nursed now, her one exposed eye wide open and glaring. She wanted me to know she had my number. Rock, rock, rock.

I hummed the sleepy song, her so-called "trigger" song. According to the books, this soft melody, sung over and over, with the pleasure and consistency of repetition (oh, the repetition of new motherhood!), would let our baby know that the time had come to sleep. *I went down in the river to pray...* Our song comes from the *O Brother, Where Art Thou?* soundtrack. Remember that hypnotic scene with all the slow-moving, white-clad church members walking into the muddy river to be washed free of sin and transgression? Delmar splashes through the water and up to the preacher for his dunking. What better soundtrack for naptime? Baptism and sleep aren't so different. Each provides a fresh beginning.

Ella and I were stuck in a movie of our own making, and of course, because I had to sing without pausing or ceasing, eventually I departed from the words I learned from Alison Krauss and made up my own: *Oh, Eeeeelllla, let's go down, let's go down, come on down...* Then the daddies went down, and the mommies. Eventually, the grandmas and the uncles and the puppies made their way down to that baptismal river. Everybody except Ella, it seems, went on down.

Instead of signaling sleep, all my singing and rocking had marked my agenda, my trickery. I will not sleep, Ella's one eye said. I will not, I will not, I will not. Rock and sing. *Oh, brother, let's go down, let's go down, come on down, Oh, brother...* Oh brother, indeed. Fifteen minutes later, she seemed out once again. I untangled her fingers from the fabric of my T-shirt, lifted her arm a few inches, and dropped her hand. The arm dropped like a soggy teething toy into a basket. Thunk. Sleeping.

I considered my options. I could stay in the chair with Ella on my lap. I had the stack of essays within reach. If I could prop up her head with rolled blankets (also within reach) and extract my right arm from under her head, I could stabilize an essay on a hardcover copy of *Horton Hears a Who!* and get some grading done. I did this for twenty minutes, making it through an essay and a half. Then I had to pee. Besides, I thought, this is absurd. *Who does this?* I am a mockery to working mothers everywhere. I am a slave to my baby.

Again, I stood over the crib with a slumbering Ella.

I had a different strategy in mind: this time, I would leave my nipple in her mouth as we descended together into the crib. Apparently, her mattress had been rigged with a touch-activated shocking device, because as soon as her back touched the sheet: bam. Thrash. Scream. I chased her shrieking face with my breast, pointing my nipple at her vibrating uvula, like a target shooting game at the state fair. But I didn't have a chance to aim. Ella thrashed from side to side. She was a crazy person on a cop show being subdued, an alligator and I was the wrestler, an epileptic and I had the wooden spoon.

Then, finally, in a moment that was lucky or inevitable, I caught her lower lip with the nipple in just the right way and instinct kicked in. She latched on and her cries muffled. She sucked. The sobs became hiccups. Her eyes closed, but her jaw kept working. Insofar as such a thing is possible when you are a woman bent at the waist, forehead resting on a pee pad, both breasts dangling, I relaxed. I might as well, I thought. I knew I would have to stay like that for at least ten more minutes, or until I could again lift her hand, release, and watch it fall back to the sheet. That gave me ten good minutes to evaluate my situation.

Am I a good mother or a bad mother? I wondered. Certainly, I am wrapped around my baby's Napoleonic finger. But am I not loving and attentive when I'm unwilling to abandon a baby, an innocent baby, who obviously feels insecure without me? Then again, is it my *fault* that she feels insecure without me?

Torn between Dr. Bill Sears's affirmations of attachment parenting and the guilt I felt for not even really trying the popular sleep-training methods espoused by Dr. Richard Ferber, I realized, with a start, that the advising voices in my head both belonged to *dudes*, neither of whom was in this room with his head smashed against a pee pad.

Soundlessly muttering curses at both Sears and Ferber, I lifted Ella's curled fingers a couple inches off the mattress and let go. The hand dropped. This time, the small, falling fist looked to me like the Times Square ball, super slow-mo, easing down the wire with seconds ticking down. Clunk. Party time.

I slipped my nipple out and held it there on her lower lip for another count of ten. Then, I stood, mother erectus. Yet a final trial stood between me and freedom—or, at least, me and the rest of those essays. I needed to fold the top bar up on the crib and lock it into position. Again, the sadistic elves in the crib-making factory had played me for a sucker. Do you know the sound the door of a haunted mansion makes in a horror movie when the stupid kids push on it to make their way into the dark hall hanging with cobwebs? Then you also know the moaning screech of this bar rising up into position. Are you familiar with the sound a pogo stick makes when an exuberant child slams the pavement, jamming the spring into a tight coil and then boinging upward with a great, metallic release? Yes. This is the sound the hinges on either side of the crib bar made when I pulled them with my sweating fingers and gently eased them into a locked position. There was a one-in-three chance Ella would sleep through this noise. But this was turning into my lucky day. Ella kept sleeping.

And do you know what I did? I did not grade the essays. In an act of restless, artistic selfishness, I wrote the above. I wrote about loud cribs and soft nipples and the places I am willing to rest my head. Just as I am about to further indulge in a moment of existential angst about the fragmented, interrupted writing that is born of motherhood, even before the good feminist in me kicks in to defend the domestic and all that it contains, I hear a wavering cry.

Ella is awake. I see her from my chair and she does not look rested. Oh, brother. She has slept eleven whole minutes.

The Shell of Your Ear

Aileen Hunt

I

One of the most devastating effects of congenital hearing loss is that normal development of speech is often disrupted. . . . Although some hearing-impaired children develop intelligible speech, many do not.

> —Mary Joe Osberger and Nancy S. McGarr. "Speech Production Characteristics of the Hearing Impaired." *Speech and Language: Advances in Basic Research and Practice*, 1982.

It begins in Sligo, where I meet a boy who becomes my husband, who becomes the father of my children.

The name Sligo *comes from the Irish* Sligeach *and means "shelly place."*

We spend hours, this boy and I, walking on Sligo's beaches. He wants to go to America, and that's fine with me. I'm twenty years old and cannot know how much I'll miss Sligo and its shell-covered beaches.

Dog cockle, saddle oyster, pale Venus, horse mussel, peppery furrow shell.

We bring our own idiosyncrasies to the relationship. He sleeps with his hands folded across his chest, like a corpse. I recite poetry in the shower. We bring, buried inside us like a warning or a present, the double-sided helix of our future together.

Hermit crabs start life with small shells that are discarded for increasingly larger ones. They may change shells several times during their life span.

We move to America. We are two, then three, then four, then five. We move from apartment to house, from Ohio to California.

II

Children with hearing loss comprehend and produce shorter and simpler sentences than children with normal hearing. . . . Children with hearing loss often cannot hear word endings such as –s or –ed. This leads to misunderstanding and misuse of verb tense, pluralization, non-agreement of subject and verb, and possessives.

   —American Speech-Language-Hearing Association (ASHA)

It begins in California, when my father is dying. For six months, I am awash with grief and anger. I'm not trying to get pregnant; I'm not trying to avoid getting pregnant. Some days I remember to take prenatal vitamins. Some days I don't.

The rushing sound you hear when you hold a seashell to your ear is not the ocean. It's the noise of the surrounding environment, resonating within the cavity of the shell.

It begins in an emergency room. Blood. Pain. The threat of miscarriage.

The polished ear seashell gets its name from the curious way the lip resembles the human ear.

It begins in the delivery room with a high-risk obstetrician and a neonatologist, a team of specialists standing by.

The priest wears surgical scrubs. He carries the baptismal oil in a seashell, hands me the empty shell as they whisk her away.

Or maybe it begins the next day on an operating table in Ohio. The neurosurgeon drills a hole in her skull. Prescribes an antibiotic to prevent infection.

The cochlea is coiled and shaped like a seashell. Movement of cochlear fluid affects hair cells, creating signals that become nerve impulses. Hair cell loss results from a variety of factors including certain antibiotics and causes permanent hearing loss. There are no known treatments to restore hearing.

It begins with the words "she failed." The hearing test a surprise, a bonus administered to newborns in intensive care.

III

Children with hearing loss may not hear their own voices when they speak. They may speak too loudly or not loud enough. They may have a speaking pitch that is too high. They may sound like they are mumbling because of poor stress, poor inflection, or poor rate of speaking.

—ASHA

But no. It begins when I bring her home. I sit in the rocking chair, sing lullabies into her ear.

> *Sea Shell, Sea Shell*
> *Sing me a song, O Please!*
> *A song of ships, and sailor men*
> *And parrots, and tropical trees.*

She cannot hear the consonants *P, K, F,* and *H.* She cannot hear any *T, S,* or *Sh* sounds.

> *She sells seashells on the sea shore.*
> *E ell ea ell by te ea ore.*

It begins with a visiting teacher of the deaf; her elegant hands plucking words from the air.

The spiral in a snail's shell is the same mathematically as the spiral in the Milky Way galaxy, and it's also the same mathematically as the spirals in our DNA. It's the same ratio that you'll find in very basic music that transcends cultures all over the world.

—Joseph Gordon-Levitt, interview by Holly Millea, "Rolling in the Deep," *Elle,* September 21, 2011.

It begins. It begins. It begins.

IV
The gap in academic achievement between children with normal hearing and those with hearing loss usually widens as they progress through school.
  —ASHA

It begins with arrogance.

  Sea Shell, Sea Shell,
  Sing of the things you know so well.

It begins when I bring my eldest child home from the hospital. I hold him in my arms and coo at him. I coo, "Tell me a story. Tell me a story."

I sing to this oldest child every song I can remember. I buy him books. I read him poetry. I talk to him constantly. At night, I think back over our day together, the mistakes I made. And my consolation is: I'm giving him the gift of language.

The tone [of the conch shell] is capable of much modulation by the lips, and its clear, mellow, humming notes . . . have a peculiar though melancholy effect, not without charm.
  —Captain Meadows Taylor, "Catalogue of Indian Musical Instruments, Presented by Colonel P. T. French," *Proceedings of the Royal Irish Academy*, 1864.

Oh, Baby

Not this child. She cannot hear my voice; she cannot make sense of my language.

It begins with grief.

Should you hide in my heart it would not be difficult to find you. But should you hide behind your own shell, then it would be useless for anyone to seek you.
   —Kahlil Gibran, *Sand and Foam*, 1926.

It ends with something else.

IV
Children with severe to profound hearing losses often report feeling isolated, without friends, and unhappy in school.
   —ASHA

It begins (once more) in Sligo. We've been back in Ireland for a year, and my daughter and I are walking on the beach. I pick up a shell to examine it and am struck by something so obvious, I laugh. The shell is not the animal; the animal is not the shell.

There are in the beach-world certain rare creatures, the "Argonauta" (Paper Nautilus), who are not fastened to their shell at all. It is actually a cradle for the young, held in the arms of the mother.
   —Anne Morrow Lindbergh, *Gift from the Sea*, 1955.

Language is a shell.

I am very fond of the oyster shell. . . . Its tireless adaptability and tenacity draw my astonished admiration and sometimes even my tears.
  —Anne Morrow Lindbergh, *Gift from the Sea*, 1955.

It begins each morning with a smile. "Good morning," I say as I touch her shoulder. She opens her eyes and lifts her arms to me.

The Dune at Night

Erin White

We arrived in Wellfleet for our annual beach reunion two
hours before check-in and one hour after our daughter was
due for a nap. "Just drop me in town," my wife said, "and I'll
nap her."

This was the strange sort of thing we said to each other
then, a few weeks after our daughter's first birthday. Nouns
had become verbs. Everything was an action. Before Grace
was born, I thought a nap was something a child took, unsu-
pervised, in her crib. I never for a moment considered that
I might play an essential role in my child's napping, that in
Grace's case, fatigue and sleep would not be bound by the
short string of cause-and-effect logic on which I had come to
rely but rather by a murky and elusive set of "if not, then not"
clauses that I failed, daily, to comprehend. That I had stopped
trying to comprehend. My wife Chris and I were now avowed
practitioners of the sling nap and the rocker nap and the
stroller nap. We were masters of the drive-down.

And so my mother and I left Chris and Grace in town
with the jogging stroller and headed for our beach rental. We
couldn't officially take occupancy until three, but I was too

curious to wait. I just wanted to see it. I drove east from town until I reached Ocean Road and then turned onto a narrow dirt road that had no name other than the litany of family names that were painted on driftwood and nailed to trees. I followed all the signs with the name for our house, winding my way slowly back into the woods. I pulled into the last driveway and there it was. Shedding gray clapboards, enormous windows, staircases leading to decks and porches, bridges leading to overgrown gardens. I clapped my hands, turned to my mother, and smiled. She laughed. We had won the beach-house lottery. I got out of the car, and while I was looking for a sheltered spot to stow our cooler and boogie boards, I saw another driftwood sign nailed to a tree. This one read BEACH, with an arrow below pointing to a narrow path through the grass. My mother was waiting for me, but I followed the arrow. The grass turned to scrub oak and beach plums and then brambles, and then suddenly there was only sand and sky and, two hundred feet below, the ocean. I walked back along the path and drove into town to get Chris and Grace. "The house," I told Chris, "is a treasure."

The house might have been a treasure, but—as we discovered upon entering it at five minutes past three—it was also a death trap. Ceramic tile floors, three flights of open staircases outfitted with nautical-effect rope banisters, a second-floor deck with suspiciously low railings. Immediately we started childproofing, an activity which consisted mainly of blocking stair landings with furniture which we then had to slide back or climb over (while carrying Grace) to get up or down the stairs. Every few minutes one of us would call out: "Do you have her? Who has her? Can you see her?"

Finally, my mother just took Grace outside so I could unpack.
I filled a dresser with Grace's clothes, lined the edge of the tub
with bath toys, and put her round-handled Japanese toothbrush
in an enamel cup by the sink. These preparations were more
ceremony than necessity, yet I had come to need these moments
when I could care for Grace without actually caring for her,
when I could set the stage, act at being a mother to a child who
needed only these well-placed objects to soothe her.

Chris didn't want to unpack. She didn't want to put sheets
on beds or find the washing machine. She wanted to find the
beach chairs and the umbrella and go to the beach.

"Really?" I asked. "Right now?"

"Well, what do you want?" There was some confusion in
her voice, although more than anything she was exasperated.
More than anything she was tired of asking me this question.
She was tired of watching me falter for an answer, tired of *I
don't know* and *I'm not sure*, which were just different ways of
saying, *Why don't you know what I want?*

I used to know exactly what I wanted. I wanted a baby. I didn't
say this out loud, or at least I hardly ever said it out loud. But it was
always my first answer. Occasionally the desire overwhelmed me
with its urgency, its bright greed, but mostly it was an even wanting; it was the single drop of methylene blue that turned every cell
wall, every nucleus, a coppery indigo. It was the gold coin hidden
in my pocket, heavy and warm and known only by my fingers.

My desire was oversized. It was hurried; it was preoccupying.
It was bad feminism. I knew all those things, but I didn't care.
What I didn't know was that when the baby finally came, when

she arrived and brought with her an end to all the supposing, she would also bring an end to the woman who had supposed her.

There were certain conversations Chris and I were supposed to have before we had a baby. So why didn't we? I just wanted the baby, that's why. I didn't want the conversations. Instead, I wanted to say things like: "Just think, next year when we drive to Philly, we'll be handing Cheerios to a baby in the back seat." Never mind the fact that when the time came to drive said baby to Philadelphia for the first time, we had to do it in the dark of night so that she would wail for only an hour before exhausting herself into a whimpering sleep as opposed to shrieking through the entire five-hour trip. Never mind that Chris had worked that day and I had been home with Grace, packing board books and diapers and crib sheets, and neither one of us was able to cede enough ground to ask the other if she was too tired from her long and strenuous day to drive in the dark with a crying child who, on this particular trip, woke upon arriving at our friend's house near midnight and stayed awake until three in the morning.

Honestly, those pre-baby conversations didn't seem so relevant to us: I wanted to bear children and spend the majority of my time with them; Chris didn't want to be pregnant, and she wanted to work. Before I got pregnant, it seemed as though our labors would divide naturally along fault lines created by our own desires. Our mistake was in thinking each of our lives would retain what we loved about them when we were childless: sleep, exercise, solitude, clean hair. Who knew that those things would become points of compromise and negotiation? Who knew that the sight of Chris showered and dressed for work, with small gold earrings in her ears and a diver's watch around her wrist, would fill me with a rage and loneliness like

none I had ever felt? We made the mistake of thinking that
when we became parents, we would maintain our perch at the
top of Maslow's triangle. Instead, the baby abruptly dropped us
to the triangle's wide base, where we both desperately wanted
a list of things we used to have and had never thought to want,
things we now wanted—impossibly—from each other.

Chris clarified her question: "Do you want to go to the beach?"

Of course I did, if what she had in mind was the sort of
beach where all you need is a book and a chair and a bottle of
water. I did not want to go to a beach that required umbrellas
and plastic shovels and two kinds of diapers and protein-rich
snacks and a sippy cup. I didn't want to go anywhere that
required a sippy cup. If pressed, I could also say that, yes, I
wanted to go to the beach where gray waves curled back to
reveal a constantly churning floor of stones. The beach with
the bobbing seals and the steep amber dunes that were nearly
scarlet in some lights, federally protected dunes that people
were no longer allowed to climb or even touch, which made
them not only dunes but also sculptures of time. The beach
where we sat in the sun until we were hot enough to swim
and then swam until we were cold enough to sit in the sun.
I was not certain that I would ever be on that beach again; I
was not certain why we were bothering with this at all.

"Sure," I said. "Why not?"

That evening, my sister and father arrived from Boston on a
ferry. The six of us settled into a routine; we spent our days the

way one is meant to spend them at the beach. There were more tasks than usual, more packing and unpacking than anyone wanted, sand in the sunscreen, wet towels mistakenly left to soak in the beach bag. But we all—even I—made the most of it. Grace had just learned to walk, and so she chased waves and seagulls and other people's kites and then ran back to the beach blanket where I was waiting for her. The sight of her running away from me brought an unfamiliar lightness in my chest, as though I could also now move in a new and unexpected way. She sat in my lap and ate Pirate Booty and drippy peaches, and when we were under the umbrella together, I took off her hat and smelled the sand and water in her curly hair.

In the evenings, we ate dinner in the kitchen. It was September, and the night air made it too cold to eat outside. Besides, we liked the small kitchen with its blue tile table and small windows. It felt like a ship kitchen. We ate lobster rolls and clams, chowder and bisque. Every few days, someone made a salad and we all took a few obligatory bites and then tossed the rest into the garbage. After dinner, my mother would make hot chocolate, warming the milk we ostensibly bought for Grace in a pan on the stove, then mixing it with cocoa power and serving it to my sister and me from a brown Transferware teapot she found on a high shelf. And every night, Chris asked us all the same question: "Who wants to go to the dune?"

Chris liked walking the bramble path to the ocean at night; she was thrilled by the steep dune, by the expanse of dark and moving water lit by the waxing moon. Every night, she wanted me to go with her. I didn't want to go. It was warm in the kitchen and quiet. Grace was finally sleeping and she wouldn't be sleeping for long, so this time was all the time I had, and I wanted comfort. I wanted conversation and laughter. I wanted my own mother. I didn't want to push through brambles in the dark. "I'm too tired," I told her. We were always saying that then. Tired was the feeling that could not be denied. It was never an exaggeration. It was also shorthand for everything else we felt; it was our all-purpose stand-in for a real answer. Who had the energy to talk about anger, about resentment, about the worry that roosted in my chest? "What's wrong?" we asked each other nearly every day. "Nothing," we always said in reply. "I'm just tired."

Sometimes Chris could convince my sister to go to the dune with her, or my dad. Sometimes she went alone. But when she asked on our last night, I knew she didn't want anyone but me. "Oh, all right," I said, tipping my mug for the last warm drops of cocoa. "I'll go."

Two years before: Chris and I were in Wellfleet, alone. We had been married for nearly a year, trying to conceive for months. I had unwittingly rented a cottage for the week in August when
I was ovulating, and so we traded the possibility of an April due date for a week in a two-room cottage on Drummer's Cove. I grieved the lost chance and I railed, once again, against the injustice of our biology and our need for liquid nitrogen and someone else's body to make our child. But my grief, surprisingly, barely made it over the Sagamore Bridge, and by the time we got to the Cove it was gone. We slept on the second floor of the cottage, in a loft with a view of the water. The house had an entire bookcase filled with old *Gourmet* magazines, so each morning I took a stack of them

to the beach and learned how to cook. One night, we drove to Provincetown for dinner at the Martin House. I wore a silk dress that tied around my neck, and we ate mussels and oysters, drank a bottle of wine. Before dessert, I began to feel the familiar twinge in my side, the pressing weight of a swelling ovary. I began to say something to Chris, something clever about a good egg gone to waste, but I stopped myself. If she were a man, I might have rushed her through dinner and back to our bed, but she was a woman, and we were in no hurry.

It was that evening's impossibility of making a baby that gave me my last experience of pure desire for one, a desire unblemished by basal body-temperature readings and ovulation predictors, by shipping rates and on-call schedules. Because there would be no attempt at conception, there would be no thwarting details, and there would be no failure. That night, the gold coin was in my pocket again; the treasure, which was not the baby herself but rather my sweet longing for her, had returned.

We tiptoed down the stairs and out the front door. The moon was full; we turned off our flashlights. I walked along the path first, carefully holding the branches back, passing them to Chris as we went. When we got to the edge, the water seemed louder than it did in daylight. The water and the sky were the same blackened silver although only the water moved. The clouds were still, suspended like decorations strung from fishing line. Chris stood behind me, put her arms around my chest.

After a few minutes, I said, "We should go back, in case she's up."

Chris kissed my head. She didn't want to leave, although she didn't say that. She could have stayed for hours; she could have stood on the narrow ledge and let the blue darkness enter her, let it sink slowly from one layer to the next until she held it. I could not. I could stand there for the appropriate amount of time. I could register the beauty of the place, but I could not love it. In the same way, I could register the weight of Chris's arm around my neck and not surrender to it. Since we had pushed through that last prickly beach plum and stepped out to the edge of the dune, I had been slowly, nearly imperceptibly, turning back toward the path and the house, toward the baby who, awake or not, beckoned my return.

Another Mother

Elizabeth Jarrett Andrew

I'm in the unconscious bliss of sleep when a child's cry rips through the haze. My heart knocks. I roll out of bed and trip through the dark, abandoning all I've been for the sake of this bare need.

My daughter is *hungry*.

Gwyn began interrupting my nights long before she was born—a feat, considering she was kicking, spinning, and hiccupping in another woman's womb. Abby was nineteen, Alan twenty, both distressed by their predicament and living across town near their college. They found my partner Emily and me online like a cheap date. In the weeks after our first meeting, I'd startle awake, then lie in the darkness picturing Abby and Alan as we experienced them, leaning into one another in the vinyl booth of a diner, stymied by the menu. If they needed twenty minutes to decide to order a veggie burger, how would they ever determine the fate of their baby?

Yet they chose us, and for five months were unwavering. They wanted to graduate; perhaps they sensed their impending breakup;

their families were alarmingly unhelpful. My night waking transitioned from worry to speculation: Who were these strangers? I tried to listen beyond Abby's gregarious chatter and Alan's shy stuttering for the baby they had created. Would she have Abby's honesty? Alan's musical skills? Would she inherit either family's mental illnesses or addictions or inability to care for their young? What might it mean to raise Abby and Alan's child?

Most everyone we knew was skeptical. Birth parents change their minds! We were cavalier—during the day. The more people around to love our child, the better. If someday she were to throw a tantrum and shout, "My *real* mother would let me!" I planned to hand her the phone and say, "Find out."

From August to December, we watched Abby grow. We trucked her to prenatal appointments. We plied her with food. Day after day, Abby wore the same sweatshirt, a pair of sweatpants with her college's name down one leg, and Birkenstock sandals. Then the snow fell. I gave her wool socks and urged her to ask her lawyer to ask our lawyer to ask us for money for maternity clothes. She bought one pair of jeans and a rose-colored top at a consignment shop. Alan landed his first job, in a café. Other than the adoption counselor and us, they had no adult guidance. I adored them. I wanted to mother them, too.

Then during one visit Abby lay on our couch and guided my hand across her belly. I felt a thump, an elbow's poke. *That's my child*—not a thought but a fierce and sweeping proprietorship, followed by guilt: I had no right. I pulled away.

Emily and I turn out the lights and scooch under the winter covers. Sleep descends, a welcome oblivion broken immediately by the jangling telephone—Abby and Alan are at the hospital. Five minutes later, we're careening down the highway toward Saint Paul. The snow is crusty and tinted streetlight orange. Downtown is strangely busy.

Inside, the maternity ward blazes with light and there's a party in Abby's room: *Harry Potter* on the TV, the fetal heart monitor ticking away, the doulas and midwives and Alan, who nervously pets Abby's hair until the contractions grow painful enough that the midwives kick everyone else out. A nurse gives Emily and me a room. We curl together in bed, with the bars up to keep us from falling. I'm sure sleep will be impossible, but then a knock at the door four hours later jolts us. Abby's ready to push. She and Alan want us there.

Abby is submerged in a tub, naked and pushing. Her hair is damp. Alan holds her hand. We take turns wiping her brow with a cold washcloth. I press my palm to her foot; she thrusts backward into my bracing; she groans. And then the midwife slips on long plastic gloves, reaches into the balloon of blood bursting in the water and pulls out this creature, pale, filmy, flailing. Abby cups her in her arms. Emily and I cry and laugh and hold the edge of the tub. The doula snaps a photograph of us, and the contradictions of motherhood are right there, already born: Gwyn is ours, and yet not.

Abby says, "Congratulations, mommies."

Ours, but not yet. By taking drugs (ordered surreptitiously from Canada) and pumping incessantly, I had tricked my ducts into producing milk. An hour after her birth, Gwyn latched onto my swollen breast and sent electricity careening down my spine, buzzing in my toes. The current welded us. When she cried, my breasts ached; an invisible cord yanked at my chest.

But even as I held Gwyn, a voice in my head recited the upcoming deadlines: The hospital's discharge in three days—who would bring Gwyn home? The first set of papers for Abby and Alan to relinquish their rights, in ten days. The next forty business days, during which they could change their minds. The date, months away, when a family-court judge could finally bang her gavel. Emily and I *held* but could not *have* Gwyn—not yet.

The hospital band on my wrist matched Abby's, and both matched the tiny one encircling Gwyn's ankle. The midwives went to Abby with postnatal care; they came to us with information on caring for a newborn. During the days, we shuttled Gwyn between rooms in a wheeled, clear plastic bassinette. Abby hand-extracted her colostrum, that first fluid that bolsters babies' immune systems, into vials she then sent to the nurses' station. We retrieved them reverently and siphoned the liquid gold into Gwyn's mouth.

At night, Gwyn slept swaddled in our bed. "Newborns breathe irregularly," the nurses warned, and yet Emily and I lay wide-eyed and frantic, listening: a rapid-fire in-breath followed by a treacherously long pause. I held my breath and watched the clock. 1:23 a.m. 1:24 a.m. Gwyn exhaled, and Emily and I rolled our eyes at each other—what were we worried about? But then a silence followed, so extended and unnatural we couldn't help but wait for the rise and fall of those miniscule lungs. We'd been told not to let her sleep longer than four hours without feeding, and so, unbelievably, we woke her. I offered her my breast and, over our three days in the hospital, Emily and I descended into the blitzed, besotted exhaustion of new parents while Abby grew increasingly perky, lying on her now-flat belly to check Facebook.

On the third morning, the social worker knocked on our door. We looked up. Six feet tall, wearing high-heeled cowboy boots and a miniskirt, she still managed to look grave. "Abby and Alan are reconsidering. They'd like a few hours with Gwyn." Her voice was impassive, but her eyes showed compassion.

Emily tucked Gwyn in the bassinet, and we silently, slowly wheeled her past the nursing station. We returned to our room heavy with dread. Birth parents change their minds all the time. I could barely breathe. We held hands. An hour passed, then two. Emily and I had gambled our love on two strangers and their baby—on a possibility that might never come to pass. We mothered the likelihood of loss alongside the ridiculous miracle of gain. We waited.

What we didn't know was that for two straight hours, Gwyn screamed a blind streak. Abby bounced her on her shoulder. Alan patted her and fumbled with her diaper. The social worker tried counseling them, but Gwyn was crying too loudly. Abby attempted breastfeeding. Alan offered her a bottle. They sang songs. Emily and I waited, our newly formed family in the balance, months of anticipation and the joy of near fulfillment caught in our throats, while the biological parents of our not-yet daughter began to feel the desperate helplessness of parents everywhere.

Later, a glint in her eye, the social worker said, "Gwyn knew. She knew exactly what she needed."

Two in the morning, one of many. I startle, dreams vanquished, then wonder why. The furnace sighs. Emily's breath is steady. I listen to the enclosed silence of a house in winter, my body alert despite my fuzzy brain's wish for sleep. I think about Abby's eating disorder, Alan's perfectionism, their need for responsible love. Emily and I will have them over for pizza and games because this is what we can do—be present, be good listeners while they stumble along their paths into adulthood. Then Gwyn stirs in the next room. She flops around in the crib and cries out.

Ah.

I rise; I allow the same invisible cord that yanked me into consciousness to pull me, naked and shivering, toward her thrashing body. In the rocker, I wrap us both in a blanket and we rock, rock. Her tiny heaving chest is racked by the unfathomable terrors of infancy, and I do what I can—I hold her tight, sing, nuzzle my chin against her head. Exhaustion melds us. Motherhood comes down to this: Who gets up? Who answers a baby's midnight cries? Who is stripped to the bone by waking, by weariness, by caring, and rises nonetheless? There's alchemy between a needful child and the adult who satisfies. Gwyn and I press our thirsty bodies together in the night and generate stuff strong enough to bind the whole world.

Shortly after Gwyn's second birthday, Abby comes to stay with us for a week. She and Alan have split, Alan has dropped out of his third college, Abby is pulling a 4.0. She's too thin. She teaches Gwyn to throw dice and shout, "Yahtzee!" Gwyn races circles around Abby. She shouts, "Nabby awesome!" and together they meow at the cat. Their voices sound exactly the same, as only blood relations can. Gwyn's personality is all Abby. With her round, open face and halo of curls, she is the spitting image of Alan.

And yet she's mine and Emily's—she's ours most of all. In the night she cries out, "Mama! Hug!"—a test of the emergency parenting system. We stir. Exhaustion weighs more than gravity. Gwyn cries, "Imma? Hug?" and one of us staggers across the hall to press a hand against her small back. Convinced that we are here, that we'll always be here, that the net below her is wide and trustworthy, she eases back into sleep. I don't. I lie awake wondering when I'll hear Abby slip the key into our front lock and tiptoe down to her sleeping bag in the basement. And who will care about her when she returns home?

Gwyn loves a book called *Mother, Mother, I Want Another,* in which Mother Mouse kisses her baby goodnight and the baby mouse asks, "May I have another, mother?" Shocked, the mother responds, "Another mother?!" She generously heads out to find one, bringing home a mother donkey, a mother duck, a mother frog. Each sings a lullaby while Mother Mouse stands by.

I respect Mother Mouse. She holds tight and simultaneously, impossibly, lets go. In the end, Baby Mouse clarifies, "No more mothers! I want another *kiss.*"

Gwyn raises her head of red curls, looks me in the eye, and says, giggling, "Want another mother!"

"Another mother?!" I respond, feigning shock as Gwyn claims her world of mothers and fishes for a kiss.

Four Early Lessons in Parenting

Steven Church

1. How to Be a Superhero

My son came home one day from his progressive and politically correct Providence, Rhode Island, preschool and informed me that he was not allowed to talk about superheroes at school.

"Why not?" I asked, flabbergasted. This couldn't be true, I thought. There must be some kind of mistake.

"Because, Daddy," he said patiently, "Superheroes solve their problems by fighting and not with their words."

"Yeah, but—" I tried to respond but couldn't. I was stumped, struck dumb and silent.

He was right. But for Chrissakes, they're superheroes. They're the fabric of childhood. I could barely imagine my own without superheroes. Their stories helped me believe I might actually survive the nuclear eighties. A superhero's problems were not the kind you could just talk about, like parking tickets, traffic jams, or subprime mortgages. A super-hero had to deal with evil supervillains, rogue mutants, and extraterrestrial warmongers. A superhero had the kind of problems that you might *only* be able to solve by fighting.

One of my favorites, the Hulk, couldn't even use words. He just grunted, bellowed like an animal, and smashed things. But his anger—his insecurity and pain—*was* his superpower. His existential angst made him special and allowed him to help others with his unique physical gifts.

What better role model for a child of the eighties?

Still, I had to admit that my son (or his teachers) had a point. It was just difficult for me to deal with the idea that he could have a superhero-free childhood or, worse yet, that he would think the model of a superhero was this guy on TV named Sportacus.

If you haven't seen an episode of *LazyTown*, you're missing one of the most bizarre television experiences around. A lot of children's shows are strange, but this one is a truly odd mixture of public service and entertainment. Sportacus, the star of the show, teams up with a spunky little pink-haired girl named Stephanie and a gang of children wearing rubber puppet suits. An adult male outfitted in a tight blue spandex flight suit and aviator goggles, Sportacus speaks with a faux-French accent and wears a handlebar mustache waxed to sharp points. He champions lifestyle choices like physical activity and eating fruit. Pretty much any problem in *LazyTown* can be solved with exercise and an apple.

But what good would Sportacus be in the face of real danger? How would he handle a supervillain like Magneto or Lex Luthor or Doctor Octopus? What dreams of survival would he inspire? His beloved fruit would be poisoned with radiation. Exercise is difficult when you have a second head growing out of your shoulder and sort of pointless if you've mutated into a ninja reptile. *LazyTown* is yet another reminder that my son lives in a world that is both eerily familiar to and strikingly different from my own childhood reality.

Some days, I feel terribly ill-equipped to teach him anything.

After watching the animated film *The Incredibles*, we had another superhero discussion, about Mr. Incredible's reasons for lifting train cars like dumbbells.

"Why did he do that, Daddy?"

I told him that Mr. Incredible was working out, getting stronger to fight evil, sort of like when Daddy lifts the dumbbells at home.

Then I asked, "Do you think Daddy could lift a train car?"

"Yeah," he said, and with no prompting at all from me, added, "Cause you're a superhero."

I just let that one settle in for a while. I let it linger in the rarified air of our minivan.

Then I repeated the story over and over again, telling friends and even strangers. But the more I told it, the more self-conscious I became, the more aware of my own shortcomings as a potential superhero. I have bad knees and bad ankles. My shoulder is wrecked. I'm lactose intolerant. I'm generally afraid of confrontation, and I trust strangers and freaks way too easily. I have more curiosity than common sense. And I look terrible in tights.

I'm glad I didn't ruin the moment, but part of me thinks I should have politely informed him that I am no caped crusader. I'm a regular guy who makes bad choices sometimes, and he probably shouldn't depend on my superpowers to protect him from harm. But then again, I figured he'd have the rest of his life to learn this lesson. So I decided to let him believe for a while that I could lift some trains or maybe even—following his example—use my words instead of my fists to save the world and protect my family, because perhaps all children need these sorts of fictions to feel safe.

2. How to Play Dead

When I was five or six, a huge scar creased my face and I towered over many of the other kids. Not only had I pulled a pocketknife on my best friend and booted a kickball through a school window, but I regularly led a gaggle of boys around the playground in a militaristic march while chanting, "Crush. Kill. Destroy."

I had some issues. But I overcame them. Mostly.

So I wasn't really worried when my son's preschool teacher pulled me aside one day to tell me that he'd been playing a game with the other kids where they put a baby in the oven.

She said the last part almost in a whisper: *a baby in the oven*. She folded her hands in front of her as if in prayer and stretched her lips out thin like a knife. This was the same teacher I had to talk to about my son's repeated references to his colon and his drawings of the digestive system. She was one of these preschool teachers who just seemed completely incapable of understanding little boys; but she did get me thinking a bit about where he might have learned such things.

Then I remembered that I'd recently read *Hansel and Gretel* to him, and let me tell you, that is a seriously dark and twisted story. But I thought about it more and realized there are actually quite a few children's stories about children being shoved into ovens or cooked in pots or cakes. One of our favorites, Maurice Sendak's *In the Night Kitchen*, features a naked boy baked in a cake by portly bakers with Hitler moustaches. And then I thought about a game my son liked to play with his mother. It was called the "Baby Bagoo" game, and it was a regular part of our everyday life. I figured it was the kind of imagination play that good parents are supposed to do with their precocious children.

This is how it went: My son would climb up on the bed and curl into a fetal position. He'd coo and babble like a baby.

Then my wife would walk into the room and say, "Yes, I've come to the orphanage today because I would like to adopt a baby," and then, "Oh, look at all these babies. I want a little girl baby. Where are the little girl babies?"

My son would cry and babble urgently.

"Oh, look at this cute baby!" Rachel would say. "Oh, but he's a boy baby."

"Ga. Ga. Ga. Goo. Goo," my son would say.

"What's your name, baby?"

"Baaagoooo."

"Bagoo?"

My son nodded his head.

"Oh, you're such a sweet baby Bagoo. I want to take you home," she would say as she wrapped him up and carried him to another part of the room or the bed.

"Now, I'm going to leave you here by the river/ocean/lake/bathtub, okay, Baby Bagoo? Don't go anywhere."

She'd turn around, and Baby Bagoo would promptly roll into the water and go under.

"Oh my god!" she'd yell, "My baby! My baby!" as she pulled him out of the water, limp, eyes closed. "Bagoo? Bagoo? Speak to me. Oh, no! My sweet Baby Bagoo is dead."

On cue, my son's eyes would flutter and open wide. His arms would begin to flail, and he'd rise up, cooing and babbling and saying "Bagoo" over and over again. He would be born again, newly risen, and then we'd go about our normal routines.

Of course I recognized that my son was working through a lot of fears—layers of fear—with this game. It somehow touched on fear of abandonment, death, and water, issues of gender, and the promise of reincarnation. But it was an admittedly strange game, one that other people might not understand. It even freaked me out sometimes.

I never told my son's teachers about Baby Bagoo. I thought they might worry about us. But what they didn't know wouldn't hurt them—unless of course they were hurt by the untethered imaginations of children. Our cultural avoidance of death and our ignorance of its meaning begins at an early age. One of the things that makes little kids so morbid, so creative, and so fun to be around is that they are not afraid of death. Or rather, they have not yet been taught to face death through fear rather than through curiosity. For my son, curiosity generates questions—and it is these that I'm constantly encouraging him to pursue. "Never stop asking questions," I say in my more parental moments. Fear only leads us into the darkness of easy answers, to avoidance and ignorance . . . and this is usually about the time he stops listening to me.

"Daddy?" My son asked me once at a restaurant.

"Yes?"

"Why do we not like George Bush?"

Silence. The sound of guilty pride. Or the sound of me trying to come up with a reason that would make sense to a four-year-old, or trying to just pare down the list I keep in my head.

"Is it because he doesn't share his toys?"

For my son, this was the ultimate knock against one's character.

"Kind of," I said.

I was trying to speak his language.

"And because he's fighting a war in the desert and killing people for oil?"

"Uh huh," I said. I swear I didn't prompt him to say this.

"Daddy?" he said, pausing to blow bubbles in his soda. "Why is he doing that?"

"Good question," I said.

I didn't have an answer either. I also didn't have an answer for why people want to bomb trains or planes or malls or sporting events, or why so many stories are about the loss of innocence. I just knew that we had to keep telling them. I worried sometimes that fear would rise up and fill the void of answers, that he would stop saving babies from ovens and rivers because someone told him he'd got the story wrong.

3. How to Get Rich

In 2006, shortly after we moved to Fresno, California, I bought my son a frog-shaped sandbox and two hundred pounds of sand from Home Depot. As we were driving home with the sandbox in the back, he asked me if I thought a robber would come and steal his sandbox.

I laughed. "I don't think a robber would be interested your sandbox."

"Why not?" he asked.

This made me stop and think. I didn't want to admit that his sandbox wasn't valuable because you couldn't sell it for crack, crank, meth, or a bottle; that it wasn't valuable because you couldn't hock a sandbox or recycle it for cash. Lately, the robbers in Fresno had been targeting streetlights in the nice neighborhoods, pilfering yards and yards of copper wire and selling it to recycling plants. More recently there had been a rash of thefts of catalytic converters from cars parked in driveways and public parking lots. Something about the stuff inside that could be sold on the black market.

My son's sandbox really only had sentimental value. It was not worth money on the black market. It couldn't be resold or recycled easily. But what if there were another black market that trafficked in sentimental value, an underworld where my grandfather's typewriter were worth more than my laptop, where a child's sandbox were worth more to a meth-head than the copper wiring in the streetlights?

If there were such a market for sentimental value, we'd be rich.

With a few exceptions, most of what we owned was valuable purely for sentimental reasons. We liked our neighborhood, but it was not affluent. There were five vacant, essentially abandoned houses on our block, four of them at our end of the street. Though just one house away from an elementary school, we were also in some gang's territory. I didn't know which one. The only real evidence I could see was graffiti tags on our trash cans. Our neighborhood was not high-crime—mainly because there wasn't much to steal. My son asked us once if we were ever going to be rich, and we gave him our standard line about being teachers and writers and how we were rich in "the things that matter."

I didn't want to say his sandbox wasn't valuable, but I also didn't want him to be afraid of robbers or bogeymen or the people who picked through our recycling bin looking for bottles and cans. We'd had a few scares recently.

Once when my son and my wife were out walking the dog, they spotted the black-and-white police helicopter—a ubiquitous presence in our neighborhood at night—hovering just a block away. A voice boomed over the chop, ordering someone to "come out now with your hands up"; they hightailed it home. Another morning, during our regular walk down to the bakery, my son and I passed a corner roped off with police tape. We found out later that a man had fired shots at a police officer, led the police on a high-speed chase into someone's yard, crashed his car, and been shot more than eighty times by pursuing officers. I wanted to alleviate my son's fears about a robber stealing his sandbox, but I couldn't pretend that crime wasn't real and I didn't want to tell him his new toy was worthless.

Instead, I told him this: "You know what? Your sandbox would probably just be too heavy for robbers to lift. There's two hundred pounds of sand in there," I said. "That weighs almost as much as Daddy."

This was mostly true. I weigh quite a bit more than his sandbox. But it seemed to help. He sat there for a while, perhaps imagining the robbers trying to lift his frog full of sand or his dad. I often tried to deflect and distract with humor; I hoped he was imagining me curled up in the frog.

Then he said, "Daddy, I think robbers are golden."

"Golden?" I asked.

"Yeah, I think robbers are golden and have three golden horns."

"Golden horns, huh?"

"And they're made of metal," he said finally.

I imagined tri-tipped monsters of golden metal clanking and clunking through the side gate—a team of them, four or more, with shovels, emptying his frog-shaped sandbox into five-gallon buckets they would trade for cash at the asphalt plant, one of them hefting the plastic frog onto his shoulder and dragging the lid across the concrete. I imagined rising from slumber to the sounds of scraping metal and labored breathing, dialing the police and watching the golden robbers squeeze into a blue van, ducking so their three horns didn't hit the door frame. If I wanted to, I could see them circling the neighborhood, pilfering tricycles, soccer balls, and boxes of sidewalk chalk for their weekly haul to the other black market, the warehouse full of battered toys, worn-out T-shirts, and sagging recliners, shelves piled high with emotional attachments, a warehouse full of the most obscurely valuable things you could imagine. I hoped that if I tried hard enough, I could pretend that all robbers were golden sentimentalists, burdened by their metal skin and their guilt over stealing a child's sandbox; but I knew that if they were, we'd be the targets.

4. How to Be a Hummingbird

Providence, Rhode Island, 2005. The rain had been coming down in sheets for nine days straight, seeping through the walls in our basement, leaving puddles beneath the oil tank.

We needed to get out of the house and we drove fast, just barely tethered to the asphalt, headed for a movie in Massachusetts, a movie about a giant were-rabbit ravaging the village gardens. The red and green and yellow lights flowered in the moist fog. They twinkled and blinked intermittently with green. It was too much sometimes, too heavy. This place. This moment in time. The white noise of water-spray competed with the radio voices. My son blithely chattered away in his car seat, conversing with his invisible friend, Tum-Tum the elephant.

Meanwhile, my wife and I talked openly about recent bomb threats to subways in New York City. We said whatever we wanted—things like "bound to happen," "nothing we can do," "just gets worse and worse." We admitted that this was our reality now. But a Claymation movie about a giant were-rabbit awaited us, and we were happy about this. We were out of the house and not thinking, just driving and living. We were good Americans. It was early October 2005, and we'd already decided not to go to New York before the bomb threats were issued—mainly because we couldn't afford the trip. But when we'd heard the reports of threats to subways and public transit, we were both honestly relieved to be anywhere but the city.

"Can you imagine that?" my wife asked, responding to another NPR update on the car radio.

"Getting bombed?" I asked.

"Yeah," she said. "Or living with that threat every day like they do in so many other places."

"No. No, I can't imagine."

I suddenly realized that our son had gone silent; the moment began to stretch and expand, distended with silence. He was listening to everything we'd said. He was paying attention to all the words and possibilities, looking for the suggestion of violence or fear or conflict because he had Doppler radar for such drama.

"Who's getting bombed, Daddy?" he asked.

"Nobody, honey," my wife said. "Daddy and Mommy were just talking."

"It's a figure of speech," I chimed in, but I was kidding myself.

He understood. He listened to NPR every morning and heard me ranting at the voices. I didn't want him to be afraid of war and bombs. I didn't want him to feel targeted. I wanted him to stay young and innocent and fearless as long as possible. But I also didn't want to shelter him from the truth or from real danger. I had to prepare him to live in a world where people bombed trains or sporting events or buildings. How was I supposed to do this? I was in the midst of a full-on parental pause, a seizure of language, and I didn't know what to say.

Then my wife swooped in with this diversion: "What do you want to be when you grow up?"

He paused for a moment, letting the possibilities balloon.

"Hmmmm," he said. "Maybe a hummingbird."

April 15, 2013. Fresno, California: My son, the hummingbird, born almost nine months after 9/11, will soon turn eleven. He's just a few years older than Martin Richard, the youngest victim of the Boston Marathon bombing. My son is a bright boy who takes painting lessons, plays the trombone, and dreams of being a filmmaker. He still likes birds, but he doesn't want to be one when he grows up. His mother now has a house a few blocks away from me. My son and his sister live with me half of every week. Things have changed a lot in eight years. But my son tells me that he still likes listening to NPR in the car because he learns cool things. These days he's been listening to the news of the Boston Marathon bombing and the subsequent manhunt with what appears to be a kind of careful detachment, a calculated preadolescent disinterest. But he knows all the details, knows the bombs were packed in pressure cookers, knows they blew apart people's legs, and he knows the bombs killed a young boy.

My five-year-old daughter seems mostly oblivious to the news; she makes up songs in the back seat as we drive from school to home and listen to the radio reports. She doesn't ask the same questions that my son asked years ago, but I know from experience that she's listening. I know she's absorbing it all. And I suppose that's what I'm reminded of every time something like this happens. Such things—these bombings, this terror—have the capacity to shrink your reality down to what really matters, making the world seem tiny and impenetrable while simultaneously expanding things exponentially until your world seems immense and fragile and impossible to maintain.

I was still a new parent when my son first became aware of bombs, when he first started to ask "why" questions about war and violence. I can't say that I know a lot more now than I did then. But perhaps *he* knew something then that we can all try to remember.

He may have been small, but he thought big and wild and in ways I aspired to match, ways that I still hope to preserve in my daughter and myself. If I could, I'd take them both out in the yard the next time a bomb tears through the fabric of our days. Just the three of us, our faces pressed up close to the flowers, and I'd tell them to remember the nectar, remember their wings, their imaginations, and the way they can beat against the pull of violence. It's a simple matter of defying gravity. I want to free them and protect them with this one fact: a hummingbird can beat its wings seventy times in one second. A simple blur of breath and flesh, and they could be gone.

Up and Above Us

KC Trommer

In the elevator, I switch from flats to heels, thinking, *Finally! I get to dress up.* I might even manage a conversation not punctuated by interjections from two feet below. My toddler is with his father, which means I can put on a dress and stay out late. As late as I like, actually, since no one will be at the apartment when I get home. My husband and I are no longer together, but we have a child, a beautiful boy, and we alternate weekends with him, an arrangement that leaves me disoriented on a regular basis.

It's one of my kidless weekends, as I've taken to calling them. I try to use the time between work and parenting to tend to my other love, poetry. This afternoon, before the party, I was at my desk, surrounded by dump trucks, robot puzzles, and various incarnations of Thomas the Tank Engine. I was trying to write a poem when I got a text from a friend who had just seen my son and his father on the subway. She thought that my son might have recognized her, but she checked herself and didn't say hello. Where were they going? I wondered. I didn't know.

At the party, over a few dumplings and a rather delightful dipping sauce, I end up talking about the sublime with a man

who is studying it. I've always associated beauty with the sublime, I say, and mention the scumbled sky in a Turner painting, one of those that yields more the more I consider it. No,
he says. That's not the sublime; that's *beauty*. The sublime, he
explains as he tucks into a pile of dumplings, exists only when
death is lurking underneath. He starts talking about Kant
and Burke and other philosophers, and I feel like a philistine.
Usually I can glide between the wild goofiness of kidspeak
and the nuances of adult conversation, but not always with the
same ease with which I trade flats for heels.

My ex is tightlipped about what he and our son do during
their time together. At two, our son is too young to tell me
what they've been up to beyond offering me a happy clapping
together of his favorite nouns. I think about how his life moves,
as mine did when I was little, between two worlds. My parents
split when I was young, and I grew up spending the school year
with my mother in Connecticut and summers in Maine with
my father. I knew my worlds well, as my son knows his. But I
know only half of what goes on with him. I send him off with
his father, not knowing where to, and am relieved to gather
him up again, full of the mystery of those days.

"Where's your son now?" the man at the party wants to know.

"With his father," I say. "So that takes care of the terror of
death!" I want to pass this off as a dark joke, but this man doesn't
know me. I laugh for both of us, pick up another dumpling, and
consider smiling my way into another conversation.

There is the tedium of parenting, of always having to think
about breakfast, lunch, and dinner, bed and naps; when to go to
the park and who will be there; playdates, playmates, and rainy
days and arts and crafts; how to pay for groceries and how to

pay the rent and the sitter; how to teach my boy to say hello and goodbye and please and thank you, and which letters are which, and which numbers are which, and what color the truck is, and which book we should read next; when he will be fine playing alone and when he needs to be held or listened to or read to; how to instruct him to avoid bumping his head on the chair again and to please be quiet in the hallway, people might be sleeping. There's all of that. But when I talk to this man about the sublime, there is also what floats under all of this: love.

The word *sublime* makes me think of the expanse of night sky on a clear evening off the coast of Maine, but suddenly I want to use it to describe the love I have for my son. This love moves above the tedium of what makes the days go and the terror that this man yokes to the word *sublime*. Even as I bring the word into my mind and welcome it in with all of its grandeur and light and pretension, I realize I do not know how to tell this stranger about how I love my son. I can't cross the divide between being a parent and not being one. I don't want to say that this love is unknowable for someone who doesn't have kids. I'll sound like an ass—although it's true. I know the other side. I know those other loves. They are grand, but they're not the same. Not by a mile.

The friend hosting the party has two girls. I called her after I gave birth, awash with hormones, not yet completely sleep deprived—and in love. I said, "I had no idea I could love someone so much. You knew. You should have told me." She laughed me off and said, "Would you have believed me? It sounds so corny."

A mother's love for her child is common. It's also sacred. It's the love that made me understand love. When my son comes back to me, I see him more clearly for not having seen him. I notice how he's changed even over the course of a few days. He's got more words, for starters. I see, anew, his light brown hair and his grand smile and his bright eyes. I see his cheer and his joy. I remember how hard it was, knowing that my parents hated each other and knowing that I came from both of them, so for my boy's sake I do my best to be neutral at pickup and at dropoff. When I send him along, I try to set the tone, telling him his dad is coming and that they'll have fun. I know nothing matters to him as much as the fact that he loves us both.

I try to take the long view: this boy will grow and be loved by both his father and me, he will figure out whatever he needs to figure out about his parents, and the love we have for him will help him make sense of the world. It's hard to trust that. It's terrifying to be enough. When I pick him up, I tell him it's good to see him. I don't tell him I missed him, nor how much, since on those occasions when I have said something, he looked at me and said, "Mommy: sad." So I tell him the truth: I say how happy I am to see him. I proffer one of his Matchbox cars from my pocket for the trip from the subway to home.

I sometimes record poems to see if they're working. My son saw me do this once, and now he wants to sit with me and "make a poem." We turn on the microphone and my son says *poem* in a parody of some contemporary poets: there's the careful *O*, and the high *E* that folds into the *M*. Into the poem we put the words he's learned that week, and when I stop recording he insists, "poem, poem—more po-em!" I play these recordings back during the long weekends without him, feeling maudlin, feeling rotten, even though they bring me some joy.

Sometimes I listen on the train, sometimes at my desk when I am about to write.

On my weekends alone, time is molasses-slow. I try to make these days matter, knowing that my friends with kids seldom find the time to dress up for parties and reflect on the true nature of the sublime. I do things that are hard to do in peace when you have a toddler. I clean. I do laundry. I buy groceries. I pay the bills. I meet friends. I lug home a Christmas tree.

That first Christmas with my son, I understood finally that all the Madonna and child paintings were about this love—and possibly nothing more. A friend who teaches in Italy wrote me after observing yet another *Madonna col Bambino* perched above a Florentine street corner. "She's not saying, 'This is God.' She's saying, 'Look at my baby!'"

But maybe the man at the party has a point. Maybe the grandeur of this love is fueled in part by the terrifying possibility of its loss. The same friend tells me, "You have to lead an interesting life so that he can have an interesting life." I know she's also saying, *It's okay. Live a little.* In this moment in New York parenting, the idea that I have a life beyond being a mother seems novel. It's as novel as it is necessary. Had I stayed with my son's father, I would never have had as much time as I have now for my life outside of mothering. As unwelcome as it is, I try to keep my own life going when the engine of it goes missing.

When my son was born, I suddenly understood that he should be loved just as he was, just for being. I understood in a way I had not before that everyone should be loved this way. Few people are. I hadn't been. As soon as I saw him, I knew I would have to be stronger in order to be his mother. I would have to take better care of myself so as to be able to protect him. When I was growing up, my sister was the only person who I knew for certain loved me just for me. I try to hold this in mind as my son grows: it only takes one person loving a child to help him make his way in the world.

Before I leave the party, I say goodbye to the man and his wife, who is pregnant. When I notice this, I feel relieved of the need to be an ambassador. The two of them will know soon enough everything I could not explain about love, worry, death, and beauty.

Some nights, in a ruse to avoid bedtime, my son will hug me, saying, "Hold Momma. Hold Momma!" as he wraps himself around my neck. I pick him up, and he places a hand on each of my cheeks and kisses me. In those moments, my love for him sings. That love is sublime. It sings up and above us. I feel no death in it, no terror of death, nor of what might annul it, of who or what might try to destroy it. It sings, and I pull him close and send him off to dream.

The Baby Room

Nancy McCabe

1.

When she's twelve, my daughter brings home an electronic baby, a lifelike seven-pound girl in a pink hoodie with the words *Baby Think It Over* in a circular logo on her chest. She has a round, baldish head and plump, wrinkled legs and perfect little toes, an outie belly button, and blue eyes. Right away my Asian-American daughter points out that her new baby looks nothing like her, but, she says, the school owns only Caucasian babies.

The baby is activated at four in the morning, making a soft, kind of creepy breathing sound. This is quite a change from the eggs we hauled around in our childcare classes. You didn't have to feed or burp an egg, and if you wanted to make things easier on yourself, you just hard-boiled your baby.

My daughter awkwardly props the baby on her lap as we head off to dinner. Even though she casts skeptical, not-very-maternal looks at this baby, it's strange to watch her with it. It feels as if we're fast-forwarding fifteen or twenty years to the mother my daughter may someday be, while at the same time rewinding back to that baby I met many years ago in China, back when I knew less about infants than I knew about eggs.

2.

In a chaotic hotel room in Hangzhou, a man handed me a pink-cheeked ten-month-old who'd been drowsily relaxing a second before, whose eyes widened in alarm, whose body twisted back toward the man, eyes filling with panic. Around us, new parents cooed, babies cried, flashbulbs popped. The man backed away, looking sad but determined. I patted a bed and the man sat beside me with the baby between us, an attempt to make the transition a little more gradual. I didn't know who this man was—someone who worked for the orphanage, I guessed.

She screamed for hours, cheeks blazing red, wispy hair damp from the heat, and then for days afterward she regarded me with those eyes that flashed between rage and distrust, humor and quick intelligence. At the Office of Civil Affairs, she saw the man for the last time and immediately strained her arms, lifting her whole body, trying to reach him. I handed her over, and he made a raspberry on her cheek. She laughed and laughed. When he handed me back to her, she became suddenly subdued. This time, she didn't actively resist. She seemed resigned, even if she wasn't entirely happy with the situation or with me.

At our last stop, the White Swan Hotel in Guangzhou near the American embassy, my daughter looked healthy and plump next to the more emaciated babies from other orphanages. It wasn't until we returned to the United States that I understood she wasn't a roly-poly baby with a rosy flush but, in fact, an underweight, lactose-intolerant baby with eczema.

These were things that could be fixed, though. Adoptive parents believe in the wonders worked by love and will-power and diet and medicine. We believe we can undo almost any damage.

3.

Our adopted children . . . most likely were in a prenatal environment in which their neurochemistry could have been altered due to the birth mother's stressful environment. The circumstances that . . . lead a woman to choose adoption are usually difficult.

For a child who has been adopted internationally, chances are the birth mother was stressed during the pregnancy; in addition, the child's first days were probably bleaker—little holding, rocking and warm milk given based on hunger. Then most likely the child was also neglected. It may not have been profound neglect. Food may have been available, but the child could only eat at certain hours. There was a caretaker to bathe and change clothes, but that woman was probably there for one shift until the next person took over to care for ten other children as well.

When a child experiences one of the risk factors listed above, the child can then have abnormal levels of certain neurotrans-mitters such as . . . cortisol. . . .

. . . If the levels are off, this can impact healthy brain develop-ment and plasticity. For example, cortisol, which usually goes up

with stress, provides energy for thinking and stamina for dealing with stress or a crisis.

—"Neurochemistry and the Adopted Child,"
Nightlight Christian Adoptions, 2011.

4.

At first, I wondered if I'd adopted a supernatural child who could function without sleep. I'd read that babies my daughter's age needed roughly fourteen hours a day. But my daughter didn't fall asleep during naptime, and she wouldn't settle down until late in the evening. Then she popped back awake the second she'd accumulated enough rest to keep going. This hypervigilance didn't change much as she got older. She also wouldn't eat unless I fed her, and sharp blood sugar plunges left her impossibly irritable. She had a tendency toward dehydration, stomachaches, headaches, mood swings, and rages as a baby, a toddler, a small child.

Even as she grew into a healthy, funny girl, she remained quick-tempered and easily triggered into tantrums that lasted for hours, even when she was four, five, six. Her screams escalated to rage, and she followed me around, flailing and head-butting me, staring me down through hurt, betrayed, angry eyes. She demanded: *Attend to my pain, fix it.* She hit me and scratched me and slammed doors and threw things. Once she threw a glass of water down the stairs. When it shattered below into shards of glass and puddles of water, she was surprised and terrified, as if she'd had no idea she could have that kind of impact on anything.

Who could I describe this behavior to without exposing my child to criticism or ridicule? Cautiously, I asked other parents if their children had outgrown tantrums. I listened carefully to stories of the offenses which had led them to put their children in timeouts or to take away privileges. I looked into the terrified eyes of my own daughter as she spun out of control. And more and more, I thought that something was wrong, that my daughter's behavior wasn't normal. I tried to physically restrain her to keep her from hurting me, but I was afraid I would hurt her in the process. I remember holding her, feeling her heart pumping fast, faster than I thought possible or normal, though her doctors never commented on it.

5.

Six and a half years after adoption, six- to twelve-year-old children reared in Romanian orphanages for more than eight months in their first years of life . . . had higher cortisol levels . . . than did early adopted (EA < or = four months of age) . . . and Canadian-born . . . children. . . . Furthermore, the longer beyond eight months that . . . the children remained institutionalized, the higher their cortisol levels.

—M. R. Gunnar et al., "Salivary Cortisol Levels in Children Adopted from Romanian Orphanages." Abstract. *Development and Psychopathology*, 2001.

6.

Cortisol is an important hormone, known as the "stress hormone." It regulates the metabolism of carbohydrates, fats, and proteins. It is the hormone that saves us in the event of an acute stress. . . . It is meant to give the body the reserves of strength it needs in these instances. . . . When cortisol levels remain high

*there are destructive side effects. . . . Bone and muscle mass are
diminished. Systems for healing, metabolism, and immunity are
depressed and blood pressure is raised. . . . Individuals experience
mood alterations and insomnia.*

—Koren Barrett, "Adrenal Health Solutions: Fatigue and
Insomnia," lecture for Foundation for Alternative and
Integrative Medicine.

7.

Two hours after we are lulled into false security by the electronic
baby's quiet, steady breathing, it suddenly comes to life, emitting
a pitiful, low cry. We're eating omelets at Perkins, but my daughter lays down her fork and whips into action. She yanks the baby
from its highchair a little overzealously, then feeds it a bottle until
it coos. Seconds after my daughter returns it to its high chair, it
cries again, an eerily real sound. My daughter sighs but holds the
baby to her shoulder, patting its back, waiting for a burp. When
the baby starts to cry again, my daughter gives me a look of pure
despair but doesn't ask for help. She removes the baby's diaper
and Velcros on a new one. The baby finally goes quiet.

My daughter can seem so competent and mature one
moment, so uncertain and childlike the next, toting the baby
at arm's length when she isn't lifting it in the air in a *Lion King*
hold or twirling it around like a baton. I keep trying to show
her how to cradle a baby, but my daughter's having none of it.

"They should make it *really* realistic," I tell her. "They
should make an electronic baby who howls when you try to put
her in a stroller, car seat, carrier, high chair, or bathtub."

My daughter giggles. She loves hearing stories about her
infant self.

"They should make an electronic baby with a poopy, leaky diaper," I go on. "Or maybe one that gets pureed sweet potatoes all over its face, and then when you're rushing to wipe them off because you're late for work, she sticks her socked feet under the running water and giggles."

My daughter laughs and laughs, looking pleased with herself, and I am enjoying amusing her, but I also feel a pang. If she'd been held as a little baby, would she know how to hold one? Did anyone come when she cried? Did anyone give her a bottle when she was hungry or take the time afterward to burp her, change her when she was wet? It used to make me uneasy how tolerant she was of wet diapers, toddling around in them without complaint, like she wasn't used to anything else. Nor did she ever lift her arms to be held. Experience had taught her that no one would pick her up.

8.

Babies' brains grow and develop as they interact with their environment and learn how to function within it. When babies' cries bring food or comfort, they are strengthening the neuronal pathways that help them learn how to get their needs met, both physically and emotionally. But babies who do not get responses to their cries, and babies whose cries are met with abuse, learn different lessons. The neuronal pathways that are developed and strengthened under negative conditions prepare children to cope in that negative environment, and their ability to respond to nurturing and kindness may be impaired.

—Child Welfare Information Gateway, "Understanding the Effects of Maltreatment on Brain Development," 2009.

9.

My daughter is three. The allergist, a pale and preoccupied man who blinks like he has just emerged from a cave, shoots questions at me. My daughter examines the little glass globes on his desk. One has an enlarged dust mite inside, another a great big ball of fuzzy ragweed, another a cat playing with yarn to represent cat dander.

"How does she react to prolonged time in moldy basements?" he asks.

"We don't really spend time in moldy basements," I respond.

"How does she do after spending a lot of time in highly dusty rooms?"

"I don't think we've spent much time in highly dusty rooms," I answer.

"If you scratch her skin, does it cause hives?"

"I've never purposely scratched her skin," I say.

"Any heart palpitations vomiting double vision brain stem injuries knee surgery electric shocks arthritis glaucoma cuts or scratches tumors ulcers ingrown toenails kidney malfunction?" he rattles off without a pause, peering over his glasses at me as I shake my head since there are no openings for me to speak. He clearly doesn't expect me to say yes to any of them, and the long list reminds me of how, despite the asthma, despite the endless tantrums, we're pretty lucky.

My daughter refuses to talk at all and even makes little baby-babble sounds: *goo goo* and *ga ga*. He peers over his glasses at her. "She verbal?" he asks me. I burst out laughing.

As we leave, she drops the baby talk instantaneously and says, "Mom, why did the kids go in the attic and walk in front of their dad's machine and shrink really small? Your shadow is giant, Mom. Why don't you like pickles?"

And I laugh, thinking how normal she is after all, feeling as if she narrowly avoided life in moldy basements, dusty rooms, or orphanages, speech delays or serious illnesses or a deadened spirit, grateful at how happy and funny and healthy she is, really.

10.

My daughter is ten. It's a hot, bright afternoon in Yiwu City, China. The big room is lined with cribs, each with a mattress and a baby but no blankets or toys or decorations. It's too hot to need blankets for warmth, and apparently they're not used as comfort objects, either; the only ones I see are ragged and stacked in a corner. A window is open, but there is no breeze.

It's hard to say what this room, the place where my daughter spent the first ten months of her life, is like most of the time. There are no Chinese caretakers right now. Nurses visiting from Minnesota circulate, offering fingers to be gripped and hair to be pulled. They bring bottles and change diapers.

The babies are so quiet, with none of the crying or babbling or hammers crashing on xylophones that one might expect in a roomful of babies, and there are no familiar smells, either: no talcum powder or baby shampoo. I don't know what to interpret as deprivation and what is just cultural difference.

My daughter and I turn in circles, dizzy, as all around us babies scoot to the edges of their cribs, some pulling up, watching all of the activity in the room. If I pick up the one with the little rosebud mouth, how can I also pick up the long-legged

one, or the one with a diaper sagging out of her split pants,
or the one with floppy hair? I finally lift one who is about the
size my daughter was when I met her. She is solemn but seems
pleased to be chosen. She doesn't want to be held like a baby,
though. Unpracticed at relaxing into an adult's arms, she
squirms around so she is facing the room, not me. This curious
baby with scraggly hair and a onesie under split pants doesn't
smile, but she does cock her head, angling it to the right, to the
left, intently studying the room from these new vantage points.

My daughter walks up and down along the cribs, pausing
to study one baby, then another. She hesitates and then moves
on. I don't know what she's thinking. Soon we're called away,
back to our busy day, which includes a shopping trip for
toys to donate and an excursion to track down the man who
boarded a train so many years ago to bring my daughter to
me in Hangzhou. He is, we learn, a wealthy merchant whose
wife worked for the orphanage. He used to pick her up in the
evenings and, while he waited, he played with my daughter.

An orphanage worker helps us track him down in a remote
village, where we walk down pathways spread with drying rice,
past a woman beating clothes on a rock and a rooster flapping
its wings. The orphanage worker gestures at us to wait as he
runs down a hill in search of Mr. and Mrs. Lu. Soon they come
jogging up an embankment, beaming. I try to hand him a picture of my daughter as a baby to remind him who she is, but he
waves the picture away, as if to say that of course he remembers
this baby.

Mr. and Mrs. Lu inspect my daughter, who stands patiently,
slightly bemused, as they admire her and pronounce her a
"very nice girl," according to our guide. Everyone laughs and

talks and smiles. We all pose to have our pictures taken together. My daughter seems at once so young and so old: quiet and shy, yet poised, carefully polite. We all dash off to lunch with Mr. and Mrs. Lu at an open-air restaurant with a bamboo roof.

Dishes of rice and vegetables and soup and meat are delivered to our table amidst the chaos of chattering and toasting and laughing. Mr. Lu keeps his eye on my daughter's plate, refilling it regularly. She gamely eats whatever he gives her. She listens wide-eyed to the flurry of Mandarin around her and quietly basks in the attention of all of these people, gathered here just for her.

There is way too much talking for our guide to translate every word, but when she does, we listen carefully. "When she left," our guide says to me, "he cried and cried."

I'm startled. Mr. Lu beams at both of us, and my daughter's mouth quirks up in a slow, polite smile.

"She was sad, too," I answer. "She missed him."

The moment passes so fast, I wonder later at how we almost missed it, this assurance that someone cared for my daughter before she was mine. Someone paid attention to her and played with her and, through such simple kindness, taught a baby that she could love and be loved.

11.

Serotonin is a protective neurotransmitter in the brain with primarily inhibitory functions.... [It] is produced naturally when a parent cuddles, holds, rocks or soothes their child.... Children who don't receive touch ... during their early months

. . . may have alterations in their neurochemistry which induce decreased levels of serotonin in addition to elevated levels of cortisol. Sadly, children who come from emotional "war zones" may ultimately develop neurochemistry akin to that of the Vietnam war veterans.

> —Karyn Purvis, "Creating Safe Places for Our Children," *Fostering Families Today*, April 2005.

12.

The evening after our first orphanage visit, we return to the building to meet a delivery truck carrying crates of colorful, easy-to-wash plastic toys and squeaky animals. Staff members crowd around, slicing open boxes, examining toys, comparing item numbers to those on the packing list. My daughter and I watch for a few minutes. Then she nudges me.

I follow her gaze to the heavy door of the baby room, slightly ajar. No noise comes from the room, only a slice of light that paints the floor. We creep over, glance inside. At first I think that all the babies are asleep. Then I catch a flicker of movement. I crane to see. Some of the babies are still, curled up on their sides. But many simply lie open-eyed, staring at the ceiling.

My daughter and I exchange a glance. And then we are through the door, into this hot, oddly-hushed room where for now, at least, there is no one else over the age of two. Maybe there are caretakers who are usually here, who are now in the hall, unpacking. We tiptoe and whisper, as if we have entered a forbidden realm and broken the rules by sneaking in here without permission.

The babies who are still awake don't seem surprised by, or interested in, our intrusion. They mostly lie listless and unblinking in the airless room. My cousin, who also adopted a baby from China, told me her daughter didn't cry for the first couple of weeks. "She doesn't want anything," my cousin said. "She doesn't understand yet that she's allowed to have desires."

None of these babies straggle to their feet and reach for strangers. No one launches a full-voiced, full-bellied cry. Only one baby, with a Band-Aid on its cheek, seems animated. It—I can't tell if it's a boy or girl—bangs its head against the mattress, emitting low keening noises, thin and hoarse. "Ma ma ma ma ma ma ma," it says. I stroke its bald, fuzzy head. "It's okay, baby," I whisper, but I don't have any way of knowing if this baby, if any of them, will be okay.

Leaving behind that baby room, I also leave behind the naiveté I have cultivated for so many years about my own daughter's early life. I understand much better the limits of good intentions in the face of strained resources. The word *neglect* means something different to me now.

13.

After our first trip back to China, what was mythical in our minds became real. For my daughter, a vague sense of place has turned into a country of shoving crowds, shiny floral traditional dresses, and women in business suits and heels, *erhus* with twisted silk strings, calligraphy and cloisonné ornaments, jade jewelry and squat toilets and placid pandas munching on bamboo, ancient cities and statues of warriors long buried underground, dumplings and chrysanthemum tea and overnight trains and people gathering in public parks to row boats, play cards, and sing opera. And a building, gated off from a city, containing a room full of babies who, we want to imagine, are all being adopted right now.

For a while, my daughter seems to relax into her life with a new maturity, maybe because she's getting older, maybe because the trip to China has given her a greater sense of security about her identity. She seems less high-strung and begins to sleep more normally, though sometimes, I think, excessively, as if making up for the years of so little sleep.

14.

At eleven o'clock on the night my daughter brings home the electronic baby, it starts an endless cycle of fussing to be fed, burped, changed. Then again at midnight, at twelve thirty in the morning, at one. Somehow my daughter, who can sleep right through a blaring alarm clock, manages to wake and tend to her baby. She groans and then paces the floor, waking me up every time. By two I'm yelling across the hall that maybe she should let the baby cry. "Try Ferberizing," I shout, but my daughter, already wise or just concerned about her grade, ignores me.

When my daughter was a sleepless baby, a lot of people advised me to sleep-train her. "Just let her cry it out or she'll never develop good sleep habits," they told me.

"Oh, no," said my adoption agency social worker, an adoptive mom herself. "Never let an adopted child cry it out. Our babies have been through enough trauma. Let her know that you'll always respond to her needs."

I followed her advice, sitting up night after night, holding this baby who would not sleep, who laughed and played, whose

eyes drooped but who jolted wide awake at the smallest noise
or movement, who cried when I tried to put her in her crib.

I'm impressed at how my twelve-year-old daughter likewise
tends to her baby. But then she falls asleep and, at four in the
morning, wakes and screams, "I think I killed the baby! She's
not breathing!"

Oh, good, I think. *Now I can sleep.* And without getting up
to investigate, I drop off again.

15.

When my daughter is thirteen, we return to the orphanage a
second time. Mr. and Mrs. Lu bound down the steps to greet
us. They level their hands, beaming, and I understand they
are commenting on how much my daughter has grown. We
meet with the staff, have lunch with the Lus, and walk up and
down streets, searching through small stores, cave-like stalls
crowded with tools and tables and appliances in boxes. We
shop for a sewing machine to donate to the orphanage. Then
we head back once again to visit the baby room.

Healthy babies are now being sent into foster care. The
government has begun to encourage domestic adoption and
the one-child policy has been slightly relaxed. The children
in institutional care are mostly disabled. In the playroom,
toddlers scoot around in beat-up bouncy seats and line up
in wooden chairs to watch *Teletubbies* on a small TV screen
above them. They jump up to wave their arms and dance. The
room is bare and stark and hot, and there are no toys anywhere. I wonder if the ones we donated have all worn out or
have been given to departing children.

Toddlers grab at our legs and our hands as we pass. One girl whose skin is covered with brown patches wants me to pick her up, but when I do she goes limp and floppy. When I put her down, she takes my hand and tugs me around the room. She calls me "Mama." My daughter, who received an A for her baby project, though with a slight deduction for "rough handling," stands beside me, watching. I don't know if she's thinking of her own past or future or only feeling shy and uncertain in the moment.

The inhabitants of the baby room lie listlessly on the bare boards of their crib beds: a tiny one who has albinism, his shock of pale hair and white skin startling in the midst of all of these other Chinese babies; babies with enlarged heads, babies with crossed eyes, a baby whose top lip folds back like a blossom before it opens to sunlight, whose eyes are curious and who laughs when I carry him and talk to him. Later, these babies will be what I think of when American friends make fun of their own complaints, calling them "first-world problems."

16.

A month later, while visiting my friend Lizanne in Pittsburg, Kansas, I first learn of the research on adopted children and cortisol levels. While we drink tea in the kitchen and our Chinese daughters hang out together in the living room, Lizanne tells me how, in studies of babies who've been in institutional care, cortisol, the hormone that regulates fight-or-flight responses, often remains imbalanced for years. She describes the symptoms of this imbalance: hypervigilance, rapid heart rate, dilated pupils, stomachaches, headaches, dehydration, low blood sugar, impulsiveness, mood swings, test anxiety, sleep issues. It feels like she's describing my daughter. Eventually, she has heard, cortisol levels balance out, often around the age of ten. This was, indeed, when my daughter began to sleep more.

I read more about this as soon as I return home to Pennsylvania. Some informed blogger moms maintain that high cortisol levels often turn into low cortisol levels after the age of ten, which seems to fit my daughter's patterns: she now sleeps a great deal, seems chronically fatigued, is anxious, still has stomachaches and headaches. But tests suggest that her cortisol levels are normal. Her doctor wants her to see an endocrinologist, but I decide that it's better for the moment to address my daughter's anxiety by other means. In the end, studies about adoption and neurochemistry remain too inconclusive.

17.

Authors [examining connections between cortisol levels and abuse and neglect] point out that there seem to be no overall differences in cortisol levels between all types of maltreated children and non-maltreated children. However, like so many biological characteristics, cortisols vary with respect to time of day, and the pattern of that variation may be different for children who have been extensively maltreated. . . . The cortisol measure is not related in a simple way to whether a child has or has not been maltreated.

—Jean Mercer, "Cortisol Levels: Do They Identify Neglected or Abused Children?" *Childmyths*, September 28, 2010.

18.

Someday, when more is known about the relationship between
early abuse or neglect and physiology, I imagine we'll look back
with new insight about our own experience. But for now, I know
just enough to thank unknown caretakers, mostly women,
including Mrs. Lu. I know just enough to be glad for visitors
and nurses from Minnesota and my wise social worker in South
Carolina and Mr. Lu, who took the time to hold and feed and
play with my daughter. I know just enough to believe that lives
and hearts might be saved through such small interventions.

19.

My daughter is thirteen, and we have just left the baby room
full of disabled children. "Will they be adopted?" I ask, and
our guide, who, it turns out, understands little English, looks
alarmed, as if I'm asking to take them home with me. "You
must go through the proper channels," he stammers.

At a big round table in a restaurant's private room, our
guide stares at me blankly when I ask him to translate my
questions for the Lus. Since we can't communicate through
language, we all mostly just beam at each other.

Mrs. Lu touches my daughter's long hair approvingly. We
all beam.

Mr. Lu pours some tea and we all drink some and beam.

The Lus' eight-year-old grandson spins around the room,
and we all beam.

I'm starting to get a headache from smiling so hard when
waiters mercifully appear with huge platters of beef and fish,
rice and soup.

We pass food and beam at each other. Everyone admires my daughter's grace with chopsticks. We eat, we beam. There is so much I would like to ask, but there is no way to do so.

Then Mr. Lu folds his arms and sways them, and I understand: he is reminiscing in pantomime.

I point at him and then clutch at my own shirt. I say, "Waa, waa, waa." Everyone laughs.

And then Mr. Lu passes me an invisible baby, his memory of the baby my daughter was, and I pretend to take her while he wipes a memory of tears from his eyes.

My daughter watches us pass her imaginary baby self back and forth, and although she is now a teenager, prone to rolling her eyes and saying, "Stop talking, Mom," this time she just smiles.

About the Contributors

Amy Amoroso received an MFA from George Mason University. Her work has appeared in *Mount Hope, Upstreet,* the *Fertile Source,* and *Alligator Juniper.* She lives in Portland, Maine, with her husband and three children and is currently at work on a novel.

Elizabeth Jarrett Andrew is the author of the novel *Hannah, Delivered* (Koehler Books); *Writing the Sacred Journey: The Art and Practice of Spiritual Memoir* (Skinner House Books); *Swinging on the Garden Gate: A Spiritual Memoir* (Skinner House Books); and a collection of personal essays, *On the Threshold: Home, Hardwood, and Holiness* (Westview Press). She lives in Minneapolis, Minnesota.

Lisa Belkin, now the senior national correspondent for Yahoo! News, has written about parenting for many years. She is the creator of the *Motherlode* blog and the "Life's Work" column for the *New York Times*, and was the senior parenting columnist for *HuffPost Parents*.

Alice Bradley is a writer and editor who coauthored the book *Let's Panic about Babies!* (St. Martin's, 2011). She has been published in numerous magazines, including *Real Simple, Good Housekeeping, Ladies' Home Journal, Parents,* and *Redbook.* Her short fiction and essays have appeared in *Berkeley Fiction Review, Fence, [PANK],* and the *Sun.* She has been nominated twice for a Pushcart Prize, in fiction and nonfiction. Her essays have also appeared in anthologies such as *Sleep Is for the Weak* and *Things I Learned about My Dad (in Therapy).* Her popular blog, *Finslippy,* has maintained a steady following since its creation in 2004.

Jill Christman is the author of *Darkroom: A Family Exposure* (AWP Award Series in Creative Nonfiction winner), *Borrowed Babies: Apprenticing for Motherhood* (Shebooks 2014), and essays in journals such as *Brevity, Fourth Genre,* and *River Teeth.* She teaches creative nonfiction writing at Ball State University and in Ashland University's low-residency MFA program.

Steven Church is the author of *The Guinness Book of Me: A Memoir of Record; Theoretical Killings: Essays and Accidents; The Day After the Day After: My Atomic Angst; Ultrasonic: Essays;* and a fifth book of nonfiction set to be released in 2015 by Dzanc Books. Church's essays have been published and anthologized widely, and he's a founding editor and nonfiction editor for the literary magazine the *Normal School.* He is the Hallowell Professor of Creative Writing for the MFA program at Fresno State.

Barbara Duffey is the author of the poetry collection *I Might Be Mistaken* (Word Poetry) and a recipient of a National

Endowment for the Arts Creative Writing Fellowship in poetry. She is an assistant professor of English at Dakota Wesleyan University and lives in Mitchell, South Dakota, with her husband and son.

Anika Fajardo was born in Colombia and raised in Minnesota. Her work has appeared in various publications including *Brief Encounters: An Anthology of Short Nonfiction, Literary Mama, McSweeney's Internet Tendency, Hippocampus Magazine,* and others. She lives in Minneapolis with her husband and daughter.

Terrance Flynn is currently working on a memoir entitled "Dying to Meet You." He was awarded the 2014 Thomas A. Wilhelmus Editors' Award for Nonfiction, the 2014 Promise Award by the Sustainable Arts Foundation, a Stanford Calderwood fellowship at the MacDowell Colony, and a 2013 PEN Center USA Emerging Voices fellowship. He's been published in *Slice* magazine and *Sycamore Review* and his work is forthcoming in *Southern Indiana Review.* He is a licensed psychotherapist who currently lives in Claremont, California, with his partner and their four-year-old.

Lee Gutkind has explored the world of medicine and technology, with a special emphasis on pediatrics and child mental health, for 25 years. He is the author of 15 books, including *Stuck in Time: The Tragedy of Childhood Mental Illness* and *One Children's Place, Inside a Children's Hospital,* and the editor of six anthologies about health and medicine, including *I Wasn't Strong Like This When I Started Out: True Stories* *of Becoming a Nurse*. His stories and op-ed pieces about child mental illness and related issues have appeared in the *New York Times* and on National Public Radio.

Wanda Pitschel Harding is a writer and painter. She lives with her husband and daughter in Houston, Texas.

Liz Windhorst Harmer is a Canadian writer and the winner of a 2013 National Magazine Award for Personal Journalism as well as the 2013 Constance Rooke Award for Creative Nonfiction. She and her young family recently relocated to Southern California, where she is at work on a short story collection and a novel.

Elizabeth Anne Hegwood's stories, poems, and essays have appeared in the *Southeast Review, Juked, Public Scrutiny,* and elsewhere. A Mississippi Gulf Coast native, she now lives in Augusta, Georgia, where she teaches at Georgia Regents University and enjoys spending time with her husband and their sons, who grew into elementary-schoolers by the time she submitted this essay for publication.

Aileen Hunt is an Irish writer with a particular interest in lyric essays and flash nonfiction. Her work has been published online and in various literary magazines.

Eden M. Kennedy works in a small branch of the public library in Santa Barbara, California. She is coauthor of the book *Let's Panic about Babies!* (St. Martin's, 2011), which is also available in a German-language edition that somehow looks funnier than the original English version. She lives with her husband, Jack; her son, Jackson; and their bulldog, Peewee.

Leah Laben is a recovering attorney, part-time shepherd, and full-time mother. She lives with her husband and two young sons on a small farm in the Finger Lakes region of New York. Her second baby did not have colic.

Danielle Leshaw is a writer and parent and has served as the rabbi and executive director of Hillel at Ohio University in Athens, Ohio, since 2002. Her work has appeared in the *New York Times*, *Tablet Magazine*, the *Forward*, and *Moment Magazine*. Sections of her recently completed first novel have earned her 2012 and 2014 Ohio Arts Council Individual Excellence Awards, the leading state grant for writers.

Nancy McCabe is the author of four memoirs, most recently *From Little Houses to Little Women: Revisiting a Literary Childhood*. Her work has received a Pushcart Prize and has made six appearances on notable lists of Houghton-Mifflin *Best American* anthologies. She directs the writing program at the University of Pittsburgh at Bradford and teaches in the Spalding University low-residency MFA program.

Becki Melchione lives with her husband and twin daughters in the Philadelphia suburbs. She has given up working on a memoir because raising two-year-old twins takes every ounce of energy she has. Instead, she's writing short essays about the hope and courage it takes to face young-adult cancer, infertility, and motherhood.

Amy Penne earned her PhD from the University of Illinois while carrying her son William—who inspired this essay—in her gut. She teaches, writes, and takes care of her husband and two boys in a frigid old house on the prairie. Even though she hates babies, she thinks being a mom is probably worth it.

Anastasia Rubis's writing has appeared in the *New York Times*, The Huffington Post, the *New York Observer*, *North American Review*, *[PANK]*, *Fiction International*, and *Literary Mama*. She is working on a novel, "Momhattan," which uses the true events described here as the impetus for the high-anxiety, hilarious world of motherhood in Manhattan.

Mary A. Scherf is a writer and lawyer. She volunteers in one of Philadelphia's unstaffed elementary school libraries and teaches workshops for young writers at Mighty Writers. This is her first published essay.

Suzanne Farrell Smith's work explores memory, trauma, health, education, and parenthood and has been published in numerous literary and scholarly journals. An editor and college writing teacher, Suzanne lives with her husband and three sons in a small, sunny apartment at the foot of the United Nations headquarters in Midtown Manhattan.

Lisa Southgate worked as a print journalist in Australia in the 1980s and 1990s before going creative in the 2000s. She now works on creative nonfiction, plays, and fantasy fiction from her home base in Brisbane.

KC Trommer is the author of the chapbook *The Hasp Tongue* (dancing girl press, 2014). A graduate of the MFA program at the University of Michigan, she has been the recipient of an Academy of American Poets Prize and has been awarded fellowships from the Table 4 Writers Foundation, the Center for Book Arts, the Vermont Studio Center, the Haystack Mountain School of Crafts, and the Prague Summer Program. Her poems have appeared in *AGNI Online,* the *Antioch Review, Coconut, MARGIE, Octopus,* the *Sycamore Review, Prairie Schooner, Poetry East,* and a number of other journals. She lives in Jackson Heights, Queens, with her son.

Erin White lives in western Massachusetts with her wife and two daughters. She is at work on a memoir.